S0-BID-751

GERMAN STUDENTS' MANUAL

OF THE LITERATURE, LAND, AND PEOPLE OF GERMANY

BY

FRANKLIN J. HOLZWARTH, Ph. D.

PROFESSOR OF THE GERMANIC LANGUAGES AND LITERATURES IN
SYRACUSE UNIVERSITY

NEW YORK ·:· CINCINNATI ·:· CHICAGO

AMERICAN BOOK COMPANY

PREFACE

THIS work does not purport to be a History of German Literature, but aims to supply a want which the writer believes to exist among both teachers and students of German in our colleges, by providing them with a text-book which will, in a very concise manner, give a general view of German land, people, and literature, and show how German thought and character have grown and developed under the influence of other nations. Great care has also been taken to locate the writers in their proper periods; to characterize each clearly, together with his most important works, and to give the most prominence to the greatest. The author has therefore incorporated in this book the outlines, act by act—a feature which he believes can not be found in any other American text-book—of the immortal dramas of Lessing, Schiller, and Goethe. German literature is so extensive, and the time that the average American student can devote to the subject so limited, that a book of this kind seems almost imperative to facilitate the work of the more advanced courses. Students often display such ignorance of even the best known writers, and of the simplest facts concerning Germany, its states, government, language, and education, that the teacher is constantly handicapped by innumerable questions and explanations. It is therefore intended to give the student, even in his freshman year, an opportunity to familiarize himself with the representative writers of each period in the development of German literature, and to make him acquainted with the essentials underlying the study of a people which to-day is at the height of intellectual life and culture. The material may be supplemented by lectures, and collateral reading may be assigned by the teacher. A suitable map has also been added to enable the student to obtain a better idea of the location of places of literary interest, and of the relative size and position of the various German states. The writer wishes to acknowledge his indebtedness to all modern standard works on the subjects treated, and also to his colleagues in the department, Professors J. Lassen Boysen, Charles J. Kullmer, and William C. Lowe, for their encouragement and valuable suggestions.

F. J. HOLZWARTH.

CONTENTS

5

GERMAN STUDENTS' MANUAL

THE PRIMITIVE PERIOD

LAND AND PEOPLE

THE original home (*Urheimat*) of the Germanic races must probably be sought in Asia. When the Romans first became acquainted with the country then called Germany, it already contained a large population. While the earliest account of these races is very obscure, we must consider them a branch of the Aryan race, which name is now commonly used to designate that ethnological division of mankind, otherwise called Indo-Germanic or Indo-European.

Our sources of information concerning prehistoric times are so meager, that it is difficult, if not impossible, to tell to what plane of civilization the Aryan had attained. But we are assured that the Aryan, although of a nomadic race, had passed the stage of a mere hunter. He had horses, cattle, and sheep; he built rude houses, and made boats, wagons, and weapons. Time was reckoned by the moon, and the decimal system was used for counting. His food consisted of milk, butter, and flesh, and a fermented

drink made of honey, called mead.   Wild grains were,
no doubt, used; for it is not probable that the Aryan
had any regular agriculture.

Long before the time of Tacitus these forefathers
of the Germans must have parted from their Aryan
kinsmen and started on their western conquest.

We have no authentic account of the Germanic
tribes previous to 113 B. C., when the Cimbri and
Teutones began to attack the Romans, and the scanty
information concerning them during this period
must be gathered from Latin and Greek authors.

They were called Germani, but this appellation
does not seem to have been in use among the people
themselves.   Some writers connect the name with the
old German word *Ger* (meaning spear, spearman),
others with the Celtic *Gairm* (a loud cry), because
they entered a battle with a shout.   According to
Tacitus a hard piercing note and a broken roar were
their favorite cries, which they rendered more full
by applying their mouths to their shields.   And still
other writers claim that the name was borrowed
from the Celts and meant neighbors.   They regarded
themselves as children of the soil on which they
dwelt, and had a tradition of their common descent
from one father, Tuisco, who had a son, Mannus,
the father of the German race.   The Roman histo-
rians tell us that they were a people of high stature,
fair complexion, and ruddy hair, endowed with great
physical strength, and distinguished by an indomi-

table love of liberty. "Powerful in sudden exertions, but impatient of toil and labor, least of all capable of sustaining thirst and heat. Cold and hunger they are accustomed by their climate and soil to endure." They had a great regard for their hair, which was worn long and flowing—a sign of freedom. To be shorn was considered a great disgrace, and was made a punishment for certain crimes.

The men delighted in the perils of war, thinking it ignoble to work for what they might gain with blood. The chiefs loved to surround themselves with select youths, who served as their companions in war, and even in time of peace added to the fame and glory of their chief by their bravery. In speaking of Germanic chiefs, Tacitus says it was disgraceful for the chief to be surpassed in valor on the field of battle—disgraceful, on the other hand, for the companions not to equal their chief; but infamous to retreat from the field surviving him. When a certain Allemanic king was taken prisoner by the Romans, his companions, who thought it dishonorable to survive him, voluntarily surrendered themselves to be put into bonds. The German had an ambition to distinguish himself by heroic deeds, and cowardice was unpardonable. If he left his shield behind him in battle, he was shut out from the religious rites of the tribe, and was not permitted to take part in the tribal councils or to enter any sacred place. They had only one kind of public amusement, the sword dance, in which young men danced naked amidst drawn swords and lances, with such grace and skill that they received not the slightest injury.

The German warrior considered manual labor degrading, and in time of peace, when not following the chase, of which he was passionately fond, spent much time in indolence. It was, however, no disgrace for him to spend days and nights without intermission in drinking. The historian pictures him lying whole days at a time before the fire, and, when sober, playing at dice as a serious business. This apparently was a national vice, and he gambled with such recklessness that when everything else was gone he staked even his own liberty on the last throw, going voluntarily into servitude if he lost.

Children, rich and poor alike, grew up in the household, and no distinction was made between them until the state had tested the ability of the freeborn to bear arms. The youth was then honored in the presence of the clan by the gift of spear and shield, and so became a warrior and a member of the state.

The dignity of chieftain was often conferred upon a mere youth whose father had distinguished himself in the public service.

The women, whose chastity was above reproach, were held in high esteem. Tacitus claims that the Germans even supposed somewhat of sanctity and prescience to be inherent in the female sex, and that they revered the prophetess Veleda as a deity. According to tradition, women had even rallied armies that were beginning to give way, and in desperate emergencies donned armor and themselves engaged in battle. No matter how much we may doubt some of the testimony of the ancients, this reverence for women stands out as a stubborn fact in Germanic character. It was the women who by their divination foretold whether the outcome of a battle would be favorable. In describing the Cimbrian women, the historian says: "The women who follow the Cimbri to war are accompanied by gray-haired prophetesses, in white vestments, with canvas mantles fastened by clasps, brazen girdles, and naked feet. These go with drawn swords through the camp, and, striking down those of the prisoners they meet, drag them to a brazen kettle; the priestess cuts the throat of the victim, and, from the manner in which the blood flows into the vessel, judges the future event."

The Germans were very superstitious, cast lots, watched the flight of birds, listened to the neighing of horses, and sought to divine the outcome of a battle by a duel, in which a prisoner was obliged to fight with a picked man of their own army.

The country was almost entirely covered with marshes and forests; the sun was obscured the greater part of the year by heavy fogs, and the climate was cold and cheerless. It was "a land rude to every beholder and cultivator, except a native." Yet we are told the German loved his forests and held them sacred; for in their mysterious depths he worshiped the gods of his fathers.

When the Germans first appeared in history they were mainly nomads, and little given to agriculture; still, we may believe that the country contained some fertile fields, and that, to a certain extent, farming was carried on by the Germans of Tacitus, for the increasing population necessitated greater means of sustenance and a steadier supply of food than the forests and streams provided. They had sheep and cattle, and probably cultivated oats, barley, and flax; but the tilling of the soil was left to the women, old men, and slaves. There was land for everybody, and we find the German settling here or there as a spring or a meadow invited.

Each head of a family had absolute power over those of his household, and corporal punishment, even of adult members, was very common; but an able-bodied person was seldom put to death, except in case of a heinous crime. Women had no legal rights; the wife was under the tutelage of the husband, the widow under that of a son, while the fatherless daughter was under the guardianship of a brother. A person's own children, however, were his heirs and successors, and no wills were made. Brothers, paternal and maternal uncles were next in order of inheritance if there were no children.

The German had an aversion for cities, despising as effeminate the refinements of civilized life; and not until at least some of his warlike instincts were curbed did he build cities. The Germanic house was built of wood, and parts of it were painted with a pure and shining kind of earth. The roof was thatched and projected over the sides; windows and chimneys were unknown,—on the whole, the structure can not have been very substantial, if we may judge from an old law which contains an ordinance against throwing down or tearing apart another man's house,—and in this foul, smoky atmosphere the women of the household wove and spun during the long winter months.

But the Germanic Farmstead of a later period is described as consisting of a group of buildings: the house proper, the *Ausdinghäuschen*, to which the old couple could retreat when the oldest son took charge of the estate, a storehouse and stable, a shed for wagons and tools, and, in every well regulated family, a place for the brewing of beer. All these buildings were surrounded by a stockade. Into such a home the free man brought his bride, whom he had purchased with weapons, cattle, or horses. From the time of the migration of nations money was also used, and we are told that a marriageable maiden was worth about two hundred and fifty dollars. Having paid the purchase price, the man placed a ring on the bride's left hand and shoes on her feet. Her hair, which had been worn loose and flowing, was now bound up and covered with a cap,—hence the saying

Unter die Haube kommen—and a bunch of keys was
fastened to her girdle, indicating that she was to be
the keeper of her husband's household treasures.
At the close of the ceremony, that religious significance might not be wholly lacking, a hammer, the
symbol of the god Donar, was placed in the bride's
lap, to signify that the wrath of the god would fall
upon her if she proved untrue to her husband. The
marriage laws were very strict, and the chastity of
the Germans afforded a striking contrast to the li-
centiousness of the Romans. "Almost alone among
the barbarians," says Tacitus, "they content themselves with one wife." The Hochzeit, from *Hohe-
zeit*, was, as its name denotes, regarded as the highest
point in life, and was celebrated as publicly as possible, amid the shouts of the guests. It was made the
occasion of a great celebration, which, among the
more wealthy, continued a number of days.

Although the wife had been purchased from her
guardian, and, as already stated, had no rights at law,
her position in the household was an honored one.
The mother of a family ruled the entire household,
and was treated with the greatest deference by the
women, slaves, and children. She superintended the
care of the house, the kitchen, the cellars, the table,
and the beds, the making of clothes, and the brewing
of beer and mead. She was also acquainted with
surgery, and was skilled in the use of balsams for
the wounds of the men; finally, she was the family

prophetess and on important occasions held communication with the gods by means of signs and the casting of lots.

In regard to his clothing the German showed the greatest simplicity. Some writers would have us believe that the Germanic wardrobe was very scanty; that the men, even in the coldest weather, wore only skins which left a large portion of their bodies exposed. Tacitus, however, mentions a mantle, *sagum*, fastened by a clasp, or even a thorn, and another garment, *vestis*, which was close-girt, and clung to the figure. The dress of the women resembled that of the men, except that they were more accustomed to wear linen, which they embroidered and adorned with bright colors. These garments left the arms, shoulders, and the upper part of the breast bare. In making use of the skins of animals, they often, for variety, spotted them with fur of another color. Simple as was their clothing, and rude as was their mode of life, we must not fancy that they gave no attention to their persons, for they loved ornaments and valued their bath. Not only was a warm bath considered a great luxury, but Caesar writes of both sexes bathing in the streams; even the daily bath is frequently mentioned.

The Germans were very hospitable, imposing a penalty on the householder who refused to shelter a traveler. Tacitus says, "Banquets and hospitality find such favor in no other nation. To turn anybody, no matter who he may be, from one's door, is held a crime; he is entertained according to the means of the host, who provides his best. When that is gone, the host becomes guide and companion to his guest, and together they seek the hospitality of some other board, going uninvited into the first convenient house. Neighbor and stranger are made equally welcome. To the parting guest, so custom ordains, is given whatever he may desire; and the host is equally free to ask something of him." These gifts often consisted of food and drink, animals, clothes, rings, and even land.

On all great public occasions songs played an important part, and poetry was greatly valued. These songs were transmitted from generation to generation by word of mouth. The Germans loved to sing of war and the heroic deeds of their ancestors, whose example stimulated their courage. "To hear of battle and conquest was the German's delight," and the ancient songs were mostly of a martial nature, although in the Edda, a collection of northern myths, we find a variety of sentiments expressed.

The Germans were not only brave and heroic, they were also very religious. "Every hearthstone was an altar, and the father of the family was its priest. Here lingered the ancestral spirits, and here the head of the family offered to them food and drink, asked their help, cast lots, and sang the incantation." The earliest accounts mention both priests and priestesses, and not only animal, but also human sacrifices. Their religious ideas were very simple; the sun, storm, sky, lightning, and all the forces of nature were regarded as divine. Their gods represented the powers of nature.

Their mythology was the same originally as that preserved by the Scandinavians, in a little different form. They had religious festivals at certain times which they continued to celebrate even after their conversion to Christianity. As the highest god they worshiped Odin (Wodan), perhaps the Tius (Tuisto) of the Germans of Tacitus. He was the "All-Father," creator of the universe and the inferior gods. Two ravens, Hugin (thought) and Munin (memory), the symbol of his omniscience, sat upon his shoulders and whispered to him everything that was taking place on the earth. He is represented as having but one eye; he rode upon an eight-footed steed, Sleipnir, and carried the spear Gungnir. As god of war, his palace was Valhalla, where the souls of warriors who had fallen in battle reveled in the joys which had given them most pleasure while on earth. Daily they rode with the gods upon the Elysian fields of Valhalla and battled with one another until evening; then, seated in a circle, they feasted and drank mead from golden goblets. Wodan presided at the feast. Of less importance were Balder, the god of light; Loki, the god of evil; and Wodan's son, Thor, or Donar, the god of thunder, so called from the rolling of his chariot, which was drawn by black goats. He was imagined to be in the prime of life, the strongest of all the gods, and continually at strife with the giants, at whom he hurled his magic hammer, Mjölnir, which had the power of returning to his hand after being hurled. The sign of the hammer was among the heathen Teutons analogous to that of the cross among the Christians.

Among the goddesses perhaps the best known is Frigga, also called Frau Holle or Bertha, in which character she was the special patroness of the household. She was also known as Hertha, or Mother Earth, who in a veiled chariot drawn by yoked white cows, and attended by a priest, visited the different nations. Wherever the sacred car of the goddess appeared it was greeted with great rejoicing and all hostilities were laid aside until the priest conducted the goddess back to the sacred grove whence she had started.

The goddesses of fate, called Norns, were three sisters, representing the past, present, and future, and were not subject to the other gods.

These were probably the most important deities of the ancient Germans, who worshiped also a host of inferior gods, and imagined the earth and air peopled with elves, nixes, kobolds, dwarfs, and giants.

The Germans of this primitive period were divided into tribes, of which some had a regal, others a republican form of government. Nations were divided into cantons, which were again divided into districts, or hundreds,—so called because they were composed of a hundred townships. Each hundred had a centenary, chosen from the people, before whom small offenses were tried; and each canton was superintended by a chief who administered justice in all causes, great and small. The courts of justice were held in the open air, usually beneath an oak tree. They convened on certain days, either at the new or the full moon. All sat down armed, for the Germans transacted no business unarmed—even judges were armed on the seat of justice. Silence was then proclaimed by the priests, and the assembly was addressed by the king or chief, and by others distinguished for their bravery and wisdom. If a proposal displeased them it was rejected by an inarticulate murmur; if it met their approval, they applauded by clashing their javelins.

Most of the Germanic tribes burned their dead; in fact, Tacitus believes this was the mode in which they invariably disposed of their corpses. The ashes and unconsumed bones were buried and a mound raised over the grave. Certain kinds of wood were reserved for burning the bodies of illustrious persons; and not only were weapons and horses burned with their owners, but also oftentimes the wife. She had vowed fidelity unto death, and, according to history, never took a second husband. It was esteemed a great virtue if she voluntarily sacrificed herself on her husband's funeral pile. In contrast to this manner of disposing of the dead, read Platen's *Das Grab im Busento*. In the Edda another mode of sepulture is mentioned; the corpse of the hero was put on board a boat, called a "Meerdrachen" and placed in a sitting posture against the mast, with all his best-loved possessions grouped about him. The sail was then hoisted, the ship set on fire and allowed to drift out to sea.

THE PERIOD OF THE MIGRATIONS

The Romans first heard of the Germans through the Celtic Gauls, about 330 B. C., but they did not come into personal contact with them until the year 113 B. C., when the Teutons and the Cimbrians invaded Italy. They roamed and plundered at will for nearly ten years, until Marius with his army nearly exterminated them. From this time onward the races were in frequent collision; the Romans pushed their conquests into the heart of Germany so that at the beginning of the Christian Era a large portion of Germany was in their possession.

Quintilius Varus, the commander of the Roman forces in Germany (6 A. D.), was a man of despotic and relentless character, and soon earned the fiercest hate of the people. He substituted the Roman system for the native forms of government, collected taxes by force, and punished trivial offenses with death. This violent oppression so aroused the indignation of the people that the subjugated tribes, almost without exception, determined to make an effort to throw off the Roman yoke.

Experience had taught them that to accomplish this it was necessary to act unitedly, and they there-

fore ranged themselves under the leadership of Hermann (Arminius), a young chief of the Cherusci, who
had distinguished himself in the Roman service, and
thoroughly understood Roman warfare and cunning. Although but twenty-five years of age, he is
described as an experienced commander, of attractive presence, great strength, and ready mind. He
prepared for the insurrection by organizing a secret
conspiracy among the tribes, and, when all plans
were complete, sent messengers to Varus saying that
one of the tribes near the Rhine had risen in revolt.
Varus marched to quell the insurrection. Meanwhile Hermann hurriedly gathered his army and
followed Varus, who had taken the nearest way
through the Teutoburg forest, and there, in the midst
of a fierce autumn storm, suddenly surrounded the
legions of Varus with an army nearly equal in numbers. For two days the Romans resisted the fury of
the German confederates, but on the third day the
attack was fiercer than ever, and the Romans were
hopelessly beaten (9 A. D). Varus, who had been
wounded, threw himself upon his sword, and but few
escaped to tell of their defeat. The conquerors took
the fiercest revenge on the Roman judges and officers
who had so brutally overturned their customs, and
many were sacrificed to the gods. This appalling defeat threw Rome into consternation and terrified the
aged Augustus, who clothed himself in mourning,
let his hair and beard grow long, and wandered about

his palace often crying aloud, "Varus, Varus, give me back my legions!"

Hermann had, no doubt, visions of an organized nation, but the people, jealous of his great influence and authority, cast aside their opportunity, and even his own family opposed his plans. Hermann had stolen his wife, the beautiful Thusnelda, from her father Segestes, who was friendly to the Romans. Thusnelda was brave and patriotic and encouraged her husband in his attempts to free his country. After the defeat of Varus, Germanicus took command of the Roman forces in Germany. Segestes appealed to him for help against his own countrymen, and even gave his daughter Thusnelda captive. This aroused the anger of Hermann, who collected an army and attacked the Romans, but without avail, and Thusnelda later adorned the triumphal procession of Germanicus in Rome. Hermann was treacherously slain by his own relatives twelve years after his victory over Varus. The historian says: "He was without doubt the deliverer of Germany; and, unlike other kings and generals, he attacked the Roman people, not at the commencement, but in the fullness of their power; in battles he was not always successful, but he was invincible in war." Tradition has preserved the location of the battle-field, and grateful posterity has erected a colossal statue of Hermann, ninety feet high, on the summit of the Grotenburg, near Detmold. On both sides of his gigantic sword may be seen the words: "Germany's unity, my strength; my strength, Germany's power."

During the centuries following the death of Hermann there was a comparative cessation of hostilities between the Romans and the Germans, but the latter seem to have been engaged in intertribal strife, of which we, however, have no record. When the Germans again appear in history, we find that great internal changes have taken place. The names of nearly all the old tribes have disappeared, and in their stead have arisen extensive associations of tribes, which we may call nations. Whether these had been formed by conquest, or by voluntary consolidation, we can not definitely determine. Among the most important of these nations were:

The GOTHS, who, according to their ancient traditions, trace their origin back to Scandinavia. Tacitus locates them at the delta of the Vistula, and at that time they were ruled by kings. About the middle of the third century we find them spreading over the large territory between the Baltic and the Black Seas. They were now distinguished as West Goths (Visigoths), who inhabited Dacia and the banks of the Danube, and East Goths (Ostrogoths), who settled along the shores of the Black Sea and upon the plains eastward to the Dnieper. They were very powerful, and made terrible inroads on the neighboring Roman provinces.

The ALLEMANNI enter the scene of history about the beginning of the third century, when Caracalla came in contact with them on the Main. As the name indicates, they were a mixed race, composed of fragments of many different tribes. They were mostly of Suevian descent, and came from Eastern Germany. After the fifth century the nation was known as the Suevi. They finally settled on the Upper Rhine, in the territory which now embraces Baden, Württemberg, and Northeastern Switzerland. From *Allemanni* the French have given the name of Allemagne to the Germans and Germany in general.

The THURINGII consisted of the remnants of the Hermunduri and other tribes, united under one king. They spread over Central Germany from the Danube to the Harz, and as far east as the Bohemian Forest.

The SAXONS took their name from the peculiar weapon they used (*sahs*, knife) and occupied nearly the whole plain of North Germany between the Harz and the North Sea, from the Elbe to the Rhine. They were noted for their piratical attacks, in company with the Franks, on the coasts of Gaul and Britain. They retained the old system of districts and communities, and had no kings.

The FRANKS were a mixture of Sigambri, Chatti, Bructeri, and Batavi, and appeared first on the Lower Rhine, but later gained possession of a large part of Belgium and Westphalia. They were recognized as a distinct nation before the close of the third century, and were governed by kings. After the middle of the fourth century they were divided into Salians and Ripuarians, and each division had its own laws.

The BURGUNDIANS came from the banks of the Oder and the Vistula. They settled along the Neckar and the Rhine, and soon penetrated into Gaul. About the middle of the fifth century their king with ten thousand men was defeated by Attila, and we find the story of their overthrow preserved in the *Nibelungenlied*.

The FRISIANS were a quiet people located in the extreme northwest of Germany on the shore of the North Sea and the islands in that vicinity. There is a Frisian literature as early as the twelfth century.

In the year 375, the HUNS, a nomadic people up to this time unknown to the Germans, poured in immense hordes from the steppes of Asia into Europe, and gave the first impulse to the movement known as the migration of nations. The Huns were of Asiatic origin, probably of the Tartar family, and were almost black, deformed in appearance, and very awkward on their feet. They had broad shoulders, flat noses, small, mean eyes, and long black hair. They were expert horsemen and spent most of their time on horseback. Their appearance was so repulsive that the terrified Goths believed them to be the offspring of witches and infernal spirits.

These migrations, which covered a period of more

than two centuries, began with the GOTHS, who were the most advanced of all the Germanic nations. The Goths were unable to resist the inroads of the Huns, and great numbers of the West Goths, who had embraced Christianity, threw themselves on the mercy of the emperor Valens, crossed the Danube, and were perhaps the first of the Germanic nations to establish themselves within the Roman Empire. From this time onward these people play an important part in history, for early in the fifth century Rome itself was seized by their bold king Alaric. The Goths pushed their conquests westward, but before they had reached the Atlantic all Central Europe was in commotion.

The HUNS, who had steadily pressed forward, were as yet unconquered when Attila (Etzel) became their king (434 A. D.). He was the mightiest warrior of his time, and was noted far and wide for his intelligence, and many German tribes, who deemed it no disgrace to serve the most valiant, flocked to his standard. He was the only great leader of these wandering nations whose sole aim was to destroy, thus earning the title "the Scourge of God." About the year 451, Attila prepared for a great war of conquest, and marched with an immense army into the heart of Gaul, but was defeated in one of the most frightful battles known to history. It is said that a stream which crossed the battlefield was swollen with blood. In the following year Attila invaded Italy with another army, destroying everything in his way. He was met at the river Po by Pope Leo, who prevailed upon him to withdraw with his army into Hungary, where he died shortly afterward. With the death of Attila the power of the Huns was broken and they disappeared as mysteriously as they had come.

Before the close of the migratory period, the Roman Empire itself falls by German hands; the Ostrogoths, who, under their great ruler Theodoric (475 A. D.), had again become a powerful race, disappear from history as a nation; the Visigoths are driven beyond the Alps; the Burgundian kingdom is overthrown; the Anglo-Saxons have taken possession of Britain, and the Langobards conquer Italy.

The four centuries following the invasion of the Huns, during which time the Germanic tribes were constantly wandering about, are very significant. They mark the age of Germanic heroes and the beginning of the conversion of our ancestors to Christianity. The heroes of the migratory period became the subjects of numerous sagas which dwelt for centuries in the minds of the people and may be divided into two principal saga-cycles: the Ostrogothic-Hunnic and the Burgundian. Dietrich von Bern (Theoderic the Great, king of the Ostrogoths), Hildebrand, his vassal, and Etzel, the cruel king of the Huns, are the principal characters of the first-named cycle, and the Burgundian king Gunther and his brothers, of the second. The two most important literary fragments of this time are the Gothic translation of the Bible by Ulfilas and the old Low German song of Hildebrand.

ULFILAS, the Arian bishop of the Visigoths, was born about 310 A. D., and was consecrated bishop of the Goths in the year 341 at Antioch. For seven years he labored among the Goths in Dacia and then on account of persecution and oppression led his converts into Moesia, where he preached until his death in 383 while on a visit to Constantinople. He was the chief light of the Arian church and had the largest share in the social and religious development of the Goths, being able to preach in Latin, Greek, and Gothic.

His greatest work was the translation of the Bible into Gothic from the Greek, omitting the Books of the Kings, which he feared would arouse the already too warlike spirit of his people. These fragments of the Bible, which are the oldest specimen of Teutonic speech, are called the *Codex Argenteus* (Silver Manuscript), which is carefully guarded in Upsala, Sweden. It is written in silver letters on purple parchment and is a most valuable work for the study of comparative grammar of the Germanic languages. The alphabet used by Ulfilas was a mixture of the runes and the Greek alphabet, for the Goths up to this time had no written language. Up to the ninth century this book accompanied the Goths on all their migra-

tions. They were the first of all the Germanic
tribes to accept Christianity (about 300 A. D.); the
Franks followed in the fifth century, the Burgundians
and Allemanni between the sixth and seventh, the
Thuringians, Frisians, and Saxons between the ninth
and tenth centuries, and the Scandinavians still
later.

Under the Merovingian dynasty (about 480–750)
Roman civilization influenced the Franks, who, although they had now become the supreme power,
had retained their Germanic character. By means
of the Latin language, which prevailed in church and
state, the Franks were brought into touch with other
peoples and thus assured the spread of Christianity.
St. Patrick and the Irish monasteries in the north,
Columbanus among the Allemanni in the south,
Gallus, the founder of the monastery of St. Gall in
Switzerland, and St. Boniface, the Apostle of Germany, who founded the monastery of Fulda, did
much to arouse an interest in the conversion of the
nations. Although this period did not produce a
single literary document in the German language, it
nevertheless continued the sagas in the popular heroic
song, which now had reached its highest state of
perfection. As early as the beginning of the sixth
century the songs of Siegfried and Attila had spread
as far as Scandinavia. About this time the separation of the High and Low German dialects took
place, separating the north from the south, and it is

believed that two distinct nations would have resulted had not the Saxons been subjugated by Charlemagne. This Old High German language continued its development till about 1100 and is distinguished by rich, full vowels in its inflectional endings.

THE CARLOVINGIAN PERIOD

CHARLES THE GREAT (742–814) was the first to check pagan writings, and his coronation in 768 virtually meant the restoration of Rome to her old supremacy. He succeeded in forming a political and religious union of all the German tribes. His church policy was of the highest order and his decrees called forth the first German prose writings, which were mostly of a religious nature,—a confession of faith, baptismal vows, and a translation of creeds. He did much to cultivate the German language, and caused a collection of old German poetry to be made, which unfortunately was afterwards destroyed. Besides two prayers, of which the *Wessobrunner Gebet* is especially worthy of mention, and several religious songs, there are three longer poems which belong to this period: *Muspilli, Heliand,* and *Otfrieds Evangelienbuch,* which show us to what extent Christian poetry and theological culture had developed at this time.

Muspilli (World Destruction) is one of the most interesting fragments of Old High German literature, and gives us an idea of the popular religious conception of the Germans of the ninth century. In it we find pagan and Christian elements blended; angels and spirits of darkness contend for the soul of the dead at the Last Judgment, and the pains of hell and the joys of heaven are described with Germanic imagination.

The *Hildebrandslied* is a popular heroic song, which was copied in a prayer book by two monks of the monastery of Fulda about 800 A. D., although it may have been written several centuries earlier. It is preserved to-day in the city of Cassel.

Hildebrand, the most faithful of Theodoric's vassals, returns to his home in Italy after an absence of thirty years. Hadubrand, his son, challenges him to fight. When Hildebrand asks who his opponent is, he receives the answer, "Hadubrand, son of Hildebrand." When he learns on a second inquiry that it is really his son who opposes him, he tries to avoid a combat by offering him presents. But Hadubrand does not trust him, since he has been informed by sailors that his father had been killed in battle. After being taunted with cowardice, Hildebrand laments his fate, for he must either be slain by his own son or become his son's murderer. They rush at each other with their spears, which glance off from their shields; then drawing their swords they cut each other's shield in pieces.

Here the poem breaks off. We may conclude from the contrast of the two characters and the impending catastrophe that the father destroys his own race in his son. Later reproductions of this song end with a reconciliation of father and son. (Compare the story of Sohrab and Rustum.)

The *Heliand* or *Heiland* (Savior), of unknown authorship, was written about the year 830, and pictures the Savior as a king according to the gospels, and likens his kingdom unto a German kingdom. Christ is introduced as a king, who, with a company of faithful followers, wishes to conquer a country which the enemy had taken from him. The Jewish cities are called *burgen*, e. g., Rumuburg (Rome), Bethlehemburg, Jerichoburg,—the buildings of Jerusalem *Hornsäle*. Since the Germans considered it a disgrace to ride on an ass, the poet does not mention this fact when he describes Christ's entry into Jerusalem. The Sermon on the Mount is well given. Christ is also made to die on the gallows, because crucifixion was incomprehensible to the Germans. The poem closes with Christ's ascension to heaven. This old Messianic poem, which contains about 6000 alliterative lines, was intended to make the Bible known among the Saxons.

Otfried's *Evangelienbuch* or *Krist* appeared about 868 and was written in the Franconian dialect by a monk of the Alsatian monastery of Weissenburg, who intended that the book should serve not only as a reader, but also as a hymnal. While the *Heliand* represents a transition period in the development of Christianity, the *Evangelienbuch* is wholly Christian and bears no trace of paganism. Otfried's work also depicts a German king, and was written to arouse interest in stories from the Bible. Here, for the first time, we find rhyme instead of alliteration.

The *Ludwigslied* (881) is the last important literary production of this period. It celebrates the victory of young Ludwig III. over the Normans at Sarcourt and represents the king as the champion of heaven.

THE PERIOD OF THE SAXON EMPERORS

THE increasing influence of Rome in the time of the Saxon emperors (919–1024) was manifested by the introduction of southern culture and by a change of the colloquial language, which at the court of Charlemagne had been German but now became Latin. Therefore all the literature of the period is written in Latin. National literature was not at all cultivated by the Saxon emperors, who had no other desire than to save the empire and to inspire the Germans with a sense of unity and national greatness.

The most noticeable feature of this period is the growing importance of the *Spielleute*, or gleemen. At an earlier period they were the representatives of poetry, but lost their prestige when literature was in the hands of the clergy. Under the Saxon emperors they became the true preservers of national poetry. They were wandering minstrels, jesters, and gossips, to whom the people looked for their entertainment. They went from place to place carrying the latest news with them. Some of these gleemen were indifferent and disobedient clergy who used their education to win the good will of nobles, princes, and bishops, whose praises they sang. They were, therefore, welcome in good society, and endeavored to outwit one another.

For about a century and a half literature was at a standstill. With the passing of Charlemagne the empire declined and learning decayed. Scholarly activity was confined to the monasteries; monkish rule was uppermost and the masses of the people were ignorant of the arts of reading and writing. The monasteries of St. Gall, Reichenau, Fulda, and Gandersheim remained the principal seats of learning. St. Gall, where monks like Ekkehard and Notker busied themselves in writing Latin hymns and translating psalms, was foremost in the line of scholarship, music, and literature under the Saxon emperors. The Renaissance literature was also cultivated in the nunneries by such women as the Saxon nun ROSWITHA VON GANDERSHEIM. To Roswitha we must give the honor of being the first German poetess.

The most important productions of this epoch are *Waltharius*, by the monk Ekkehard, about 930, and the works of Roswitha, which consist of a life of Otto the Great, some legends, and six comedies in Latin. Most of her works are of a religious character and represent the life of Christians of the fifth and sixth centuries.

THE WALTHARILIED

Three children live as hostages at the court of Etzel, the king of the Huns; Walther, the son of the king of the Visigoths, Hildegunde, the daughter of the Burgundian king, and Hagen, the cousin of the king of the Franks. Walther and Hagen surpass all the Huns in skill and courage, and Hildegunde wins the favor of the queen and becomes the keeper of her treasures. When, on learning of the death of the old king of the Franks, Hagen makes his escape, a desire to return home is also awakened in Walther and Hildegunde; he reminds her of the fact that they were once intended for each other, and together they plan a way of escape. She secures the king's coat of mail and some of his treasures, while Walther arranges a feast; then, when the king and his men are drunk, he steals the fleetest horse out of the stable and carries Hildegunde away.

In forty days the fugitives come to the Rhine opposite Worms. Walther gives the ferryman two fish from the Danube for carrying them across. When the boatman tells King Gunther how he obtained these fish, which are served on the royal table, Hagen surmises who the fugitives are. The king believes this to be a good opportunity to recover the treasure which his father had paid the Huns, and sets out with twelve of his best heroes, among whom is Hagen, to overtake them. Meanwhile Walther has taken refuge in a ravine, which is protected by rocks and bushes. He has been on the watch while Hildegunde sleeps, but now as she watches while he takes a much needed rest, she is startled by the approach of armed knights, whom Walther recognizes as Franks.

Hagen had advised Gunther to seek, at first, an amicable adjustment of their difficulty, but the king is not satisfied with the hundred gold buckles which Walther offers him. When Walther consents to give him two hundred, he demands the treasures together with the maiden. The king's messenger is then slain. Seven other heroes also sacrifice their lives. Then, by means of a three-pronged spear, to which a rope is fastened, three others try to draw their enemy out of the ravine, but they, too, are killed.

Hagen is now to avenge the slain. He delays long on account of his friendship for his youthful companions, but fidelity to his king demands it. The next day Walther and Hildegunde start on their journey through the forest. When night overtakes them, Walther bars the entrance to the cave in which they have taken refuge, takes off his armor, and refreshes himself with food and drink.

Then, as he sleeps, Hildegunde sings to keep awake and watch. Toward morning Walther arises, to let his companion sleep, and prepares for the journey.

They have gone but a little way when Hildegunde notices Gunther and Hagen behind them. Although Walther reminds Hagen of their former friendship, he is compelled to contend with both of them. The struggle lasts long and waxes hot, until Walther at last cuts off Gunther's right leg. As Walther makes another attempt at Hagen, his sword breaks, and Hagen cuts off his right hand. But when Walther seizes his short sword with his left hand and deprives Hagen of an eye and six teeth, they are all ready to stop. Hildegunde binds up their wounds and returns home with Walther, who marries her and rules for thirty years over the Goths.

During the brief period of the Salians (1024–1125), the church reached the zenith of her power. After she had succeeded in the struggle against Henry IV., she attracted the attention of the world to the conquest of the Holy Land and thus absorbed all the strength of the nation. In literature the clergy continued to be the leading representatives, although the gleemen sang of the events of the day and recast older sagas. The clerical writers took their material principally from the Bible and from legends, but when it became necessary to interest the knights in the crusades, they chose secular subjects.

Ruodlieb, the oldest novel in German literature, written by a monk of the monastery of Tegernsee, represents the beginnings of chivalry. The gleemen, like the clergy, made use of all the literary material at hand, and thus originated the first German Beast Epic, *Reinhart*, from the French, by an Alsatian writer, HEINRICH DER GLICHESÄRE. The two most important minstrel songs of this time are *Herzog Ernst* and *König Rother*. The former describes the wonderful adventures of the Duke of Schwaben on a crusade to the Holy Land. *König Rother* is divided into two parts.

KÖNIG ROTHER

1. ROTHER'S SEARCH FOR A BRIDE. King Rother, who lives in Lower Italy, sends twelve heroes to sue for the hand of the daughter of the emperor Constantine in Constantinople. After waiting in vain a whole year for the return of his messengers, he himself concludes to go to Greece with a powerful army to free his comrades and, if necessary, to abduct the princess by force. Arriving in Constantinople, he disguises himself as Prince Dietrich, who has been banished from his country by King Rother, and offers the emperor his services. The young daughter of Constantine, who has vainly tried to see the hero, requests him to visit her. He sends her two shoes, one of gold and the other of silver; but since both are for the left foot he accepts the invitation, fits the proper shoes to her feet, at the same time confessing to the maiden that he is King Rother. On the following day he makes himself known to his imprisoned companions by a song. Shortly afterward he defeats the enemies of the emperor, and is to bring the news to the empress; he tells her, however, that Constantine has been defeated, and, when the terrified women hasten to the seashore to escape across the sea, he carries the princess away.

2. ROTHER'S EXPEDITION. When Constantine learns of this abduction he sends a gleeman to bring back his daughter. He lands in Bari during Rother's absence, lures the young queen upon his ship and escapes with her to Constantinople, where she is to be betrothed to the son of the king of Babylon. King Rother, who has hastened after them with an army of thirty thousand men, conceals his army in a forest near Constantinople, and enters the city disguised as a pilgrim. The wedding feast is being celebrated,

and Rother succeeds in placing his ring in his wife's goblet. He soon after makes himself publicly known as King Rother, is fettered and condemned to death. He is granted the privilege of being hanged in the forest, whither all follow him; but, when once in the forest, Rother blows his horn, which he has concealed under his mantle; his followers hasten to the rescue, the Babylonians are slaughtered, and the son of the Babylonian king is hanged in place of Rother. After a reconciliation with the emperor, Rother and his wife return to Bari.

THE PERIOD OF THE HOHENSTAUFEN

IT remained for the eleventh century to produce a national culture, to revive the German heroic song and to introduce a new epoch in the history of German literature. About the year 1100 changes developed in the language which divide the Middle High German from the Old High German, so that we can safely say that from the close of the eleventh century the Middle High German is the literary language of the German people. Knighthood, too, was unfolding in all its splendor and began to assert itself. Chivalry not only meant military service, but stood also for all that was noble and refined, and was the type of true manhood. It was at this time that French influence was manifest in all departments of life, and strong and free cities were springing into power. The religious spirit was consecrated to the deliverance of the Holy Sepulcher and a struggle for secular power ensued between the clergy and the laity. "The influence of the Crusades on the social and intellectual life of Europe can hardly be overestimated." They brought knighthood to perfection and reconciled the national spirit with Christianity. Through them the wonders of the Orient were opened to Europe and a new element was introduced into popular poetry.

The *Alexanderlied* and the *Rolandslied* are representative productions of the new poetry of knighthood, and are taken from French sources. The former relates in a fairylike manner the deeds of Alexander the Great in Asia, and the latter represents the Spanish campaign of Charlemagne as a crusade against the heathen. German poetry during the reign of the Hohenstaufen (1138–1254) was "more splendid," Carlyle says, "than the Troubadour period of any other nation." We may divide the literature of this period into four classes: 1. The Popular Epics. 2. The Epics of Chivalry. 3. The Lyric Poetry of the Courts. 4. Didactic Poetry.

1. THE POPULAR EPICS

The most popular epic is the *Nibelungenlied*. Its origin must be sought in the old Germanic sagas and the Edda. It came to us in its present form (about the year 1200) considerably changed and revised, but still retains its mythical and historical character. The author is unknown. The *Nibelungenlied* is composed of thirty-nine cantos and is divided into two parts: Siegfried's death and Kriemhild's revenge.

THE NIBELUNGENLIED

1. SIEGFRIED'S DEATH. King Gunther lives with his brothers Gernot and Giselher, his mother Ute, and his sister Kriemhild, at Worms on the Rhine. The most prominent among his vassals are Hagen of Tronje, Hagen's brother Dankwart, and his friend

Volker, the gleeman. Kriemhild dreams that a falcon which she has reared is torn to pieces before her eyes by two eagles. Her mother, who interprets the dream, tells her the falcon is her future husband, whom she is destined to lose. At Xanten on the Rhine in the Netherlands lives Siegfried, the son of Siegmund and Sieglinde, who is the picture of manly beauty and strength. When he hears of the fame and power of the Burgundian kings and of the virtues of Kriemhild, he sets out to win her. After a journey of six days, accompanied by only twelve heroes, he arrives at Worms and challenges the princes to a contest; but Hagen, who alone surmises that he is Siegfried, who slew the dragon and bathed in his blood, advises them to receive him kindly, and Siegfried remains as a guest at Gunther's court.

After some time news reaches Worms that the kings Lüdeger of Saxony and Lüdegast of Denmark have invaded Burgundy. This affords Siegfried an opportunity to win the favor of King Gunther, for he captures Lüdegast, and compels Lüdeger to follow him as a hostage to Worms. At the celebration which follows this victory, Siegfried first meets Kriemhild, who thanks him for the service he has done her brother, to which he graciously replies that it was done for her sake.

At Isenstein, far over the sea, lives the powerful queen Brunhild. He who would win her must surpass her in three contests— spear-throwing, stone-hurling, and leaping; whoever is defeated forfeits his life. It is Gunther's ambition to win Brunhild, but he does not dare to undertake it without Siegfried's help. Siegfried promises his assistance on condition that Gunther will give him his sister Kriemhild, to which Gunther gladly consents, and the heroes depart. Siegfried alone knows Brunhild's country, and the queen knows Siegfried. She inquires into his mission and learns that Gunther has come to woo her, and that Siegfried is his vassal. While preparations for the contest are being made, Siegfried veils himself in the "Tarnkappe," which he had wrested from the dwarf Alberich, and which has the power of making the wearer invisible, takes his place at Gunther's side, and assists him in defeating Brunhild in all three tests.

Soon thereafter a double wedding takes place in Worms; but when Brunhild sees Siegfried at the side of Kriemhild, envy and jealousy fill her heart, and she is very unhappy. That night she struggles with her husband, binds his hands and feet and hangs him up on the wall. Gunther again calls Siegfried to his assistance; he subdues the angry queen and takes from her as trophies a ring and a girdle, which he gives to Kriemhild. He then returns with his wife to the Netherlands, where he rules for ten years.

During this time Brunhild has often expressed a desire to see Kriemhild and Siegfried, and therefore sends messengers to invite them to come to Worms, where a great feast and tournaments are arranged in their honor. During one of the contests Kriemhild boasts of her husband's prowess, which awakens anew the long cherished jealousy, and Brunhild reproves her, saying that Siegfried is Gunther's vassal. Kriemhild tries to assuage her anger, but in vain. One day when they go to the cathedral the trouble breaks out afresh. Kriemhild claims the honor of entering first, but Brunhild says: "Stand back, the vassal's wife shall never precede the queen!" Greatly excited, Kriemhild shows Brunhild the ring and the girdle which Siegfried had taken from her; this so offends Brunhild that she resolves to seek revenge.

Hagen is chosen to murder Siegfried. To carry out the plan, a new invasion of the Saxons is feigned to lure Siegfried away from the court. Hagen induces Kriemhild to indicate the one vulnerable spot on Siegfried's body by sewing a little cross on his coat so that he may know where to protect him in battle. Meanwhile the enemy has apparently withdrawn, and a hunting party is organized. Siegfried succeeds in capturing a bear, and a great feast is prepared in the forest. Heated by the chase and having neglected to bring wine with them, they race to a spring; Siegfried reaches it first, but courteously waits for Gunther to drink. As Siegfried stoops to drink, Hagen thrusts his spear through the spot marked by the cross, and the hero dies, commending his wife to her brother's care. All regret the deed except Hagen, who increases Kriemhild's sorrow by placing the body of her husband before her door the next morning.

Siegfried's vassals are restrained from taking revenge on the murderer through the intercession of Kriemhild, although she is convinced that Hagen is guilty, for when he approaches the bier, Siegfried's wounds bleed afresh. Kriemhild is inconsolable, and only after three years becomes reconciled to her brother Gunther, who induces her to bring the great Nibelung treasure, her dowry, to Worms, where Hagen gets possession of it and sinks it in the Rhine.

2. KRIEMHILD'S REVENGE. Kriemhild has mourned the death of her husband thirteen years, when Etzel, the king of the Huns, sends the margrave Rüdiger of Bechlarn to woo her for him. After Rüdiger has promised to avenge any wrong done to her she consents to marry Etzel. Escorted by the margrave she journeys to the land of the Huns, is met by Etzel at Tulln on the Danube, celebrates her wedding in Vienna, and then takes up her residence in Etzelburg (Budapest). Years pass and a son is born, who is named Ortlieb, but Kriemhild can not forget Siegfried. She requests Etzel to invite the Burgundians to visit them and the invitation is accepted, notwithstanding the opposition of Hagen and of Queen Ute, who is warned by evil dreams. Led by Hagen, the Burgundians experience difficulty in crossing the Rhine, and are warned by a mermaid to return, for none, says she, except the chaplain of the king, will ever see his home-land again. Hagen then pitches the chaplain overboard, but he swims back to the shore, fulfilling the prophecy of the mermaid. When all the Burgundians are safely landed, Hagen destroys the boat, so that none can return. They are repeatedly warned on their journey that the day of revenge is near, but Rüdiger, who has received them hospitably at Bechlarn, dissipates all fear and anxiety by the betrothal of his daughter to Giselher, Gunther's brother. Dietrich von Bern, one of Etzel's vassals, who has come to meet them, again warns them, saying that Kriemhild still mourns for Siegfried, but, disregarding all advice and warning, they reach Etzel's court.

Etzel, who is not aware of Kriemhild's evil intentions, has made very hospitable preparations for the entertainment of the Nibelungs, but Kriemhild receives them coldly; only for Giselher, her youngest brother, has she a kiss. When she asks Hagen why he has not brought her treasure with him, he makes an insolent reply, and even defiantly admits that he is the murderer of Siegfried. He places Siegfried's sword across his knee and challenges any one, "Weib oder Mann," to avenge the murder. Night comes on and the Nibelungs retire, but Hagen and the minstrel Volker keep watch all night at the door of the hall, and when the stealthily approaching Huns see their helmets shining through the night, they are frightened away. The next day the guests go armed to mass and afterward attend a tournament.

Meanwhile Kriemhild has ineffectually sought the services of Dietrich von Bern. She now appeals to Etzel's brother Blödelin, who falls upon the Burgundian vassals, and a great slaughter ensues, from which only Dankwart escapes to carry the news to his brother. Hagen at once begins the work of revenge by striking off the head of little Ortlieb, so that it rolls into Kriemhild's lap. Without avail Gunther, Gernot, and Giselher try to stop the terrible struggle. Kriemhild and Etzel escape, and Rüdiger, who has been kind to the Burgundians, is permitted to withdraw with his five hundred men. The contest rages until evening, when the weary Burgundians seek peace; this they can secure only by surrendering Hagen, which they refuse to do, and the raging queen gives orders to set the great hall on fire. Throughout the night the heroes protect themselves from the falling timbers with their shields, and quench their thirst with the blood of the slain. In the morning they again bid defiance to their enemies. Rüdiger's heart is torn by conflicting emotions, and he sorrowfully watches the struggle, still hoping that he may remain neutral; but when Kriemhild reminds him of his promise to serve her, his duty as vassal leads him, very reluctantly, to break faith with the Burgundians, whom he and his men now attack. Rüdiger seems invincible until he comes upon Gernot, who deals him a fatal wound, and all his vassals are also slain. When Hildebrand demands the body of the margrave, he is laughed to scorn, but finally rushes into the contest with fury, kills Volker, and is himself wounded by Hagen. Dankwart and Giselher are also killed. Dietrich now offers the two remaining Burgundians, Gunther and Hagen, a safe return home if they will surrender; but in vain. The conclusion is a dreadful tale of carnage. Dietrich wounds Gunther and Hagen, and leads them bound to Kriemhild, who has them put in prison. Again she tries to induce Hagen to restore to her the Nibelung treasure, but he declares that he will never reveal the secret as long as one of his lords survives. The revengeful queen then has her brother beheaded, and when Hagen still refuses she cuts off his head with

Siegfried's own sword. Fearfully angered at such a sight, old Hildebrand rushes at Kriemhild and puts her to death also.

GUDRUN

The Gudrunsaga, like the Nibelungensaga, has a mythological and historical background. The struggles concerning Gudrun point back to the eighth and the three succeeding centuries, when the Normans made marauding expeditions to the maritime countries of Europe. In the twelfth century the old sagas of *Hilde* and *Gudrun* were transferred from the North Sea to South Germany, where they were revised by an unknown poet. In the thirteenth century the story of *Hagen* was added, and in this enlarged form the *Gudrunlied* has come down to the present time.

HAGEN, the son of King Sigebant of Ireland, is carried away by a griffin to a lonely island, where he grows up in the company of three royal maidens who have likewise been brought here by a griffin, and from whom he learns to satisfy his hunger with herbs and roots. With weapons which he has taken from an armed sailor whose body has been washed ashore from a stranded vessel, Hagen kills the griffin and later hails a passing ship, which takes him and the maidens home. Hagen's parents recognize their son by a golden cross which he wears on his breast, and when he has grown to manhood he assumes control of a kingdom and marries Hilde, the most beautiful of the maidens. Their daughter, likewise called Hilde, is so beautiful that she is wooed by all the princes of the neighboring countries; but her father considers none good enough for her, and has their messengers put to death. Finally, Hettel, king of the Hegelingen, hears of the beautiful maiden, and sends three of his vassals, Frute, Horand, and the grim Wate, to make his suit known.   Disguised as merchants, they succeed in concealing from Hagen the real purpose of their visit.   Their costly wares attract so much attention that Hilde induces her father to invite them to the court.   Horand wins Hilde's favor by his singing, which is so sweet that birds and beasts stop to listen. She invites him into her apartments, and there he makes his mission known.   Hilde is not unwilling to marry Hettel, but, fearing her father's wrath, consents to be carried away by stratagem.   The strangers declare that the time for their departure has come, and the court is invited to visit their ships and see their wares; but as soon as Hilde and her women step on board the sails are hoisted and the ships sail away, leaving Hagen in wrath upon the shore. The messengers reach their destination and Hilde is kindly received by Hettel.   But their joy is of short duration, for, on the following morning, Hagen's ships are seen approaching, and soon a fierce battle rages.   When Hilde sees her father hard pressed by Wate, she begs Hettel to separate them.   A reconciliation follows, and after twelve days Hagen departs.

Hilde bears Hettel two children, a son, Ortwin, and a daughter, Gudrun, who surpasses even her mother in beauty, and is in consequence jealously guarded by her parents.   Many kings sue for her hand.   Among the rejected suitors are Siegfried of Morland, and Hartmut, son of Ludwig of Normandy and his ambitious wife Gerlind.   King Herwig of Seeland, who also woos Gudrun, is not so easily dismissed, for one morning he surprises King Hettel by approaching with an army to storm his castle.   When the combat grows hot, Gudrun interposes.   Herwig's courage has won Gudrun's heart and she is betrothed to him.   When Siegfried hears of this, he makes war upon Herwig, who is saved from defeat by the timely arrival of King Hettel.   Hartmut meanwhile seizes this opportunity to carry Gudrun and her maidens away to Normandy.   Hettel quickly makes peace with Siegfried and hastens after the robbers, whom he overtakes at the island of Wülpensand, where a terrible battle takes place, in which Gudrun's father is slain by King Ludwig, and the Normans escape in the night with their captives.   Wate and Ortwin wish to pursue them to Normandy, but Frute convinces them that the distance is too great, and their number too small for such an undertaking, and the Hegelingen sorrowfully return home to wait until another generation has grown up to swell their ranks.

When King Ludwig nears the coast of Normandy he again presses Gudrun to marry his son, but she remains firm in her resolve to be true to Herwig, which so angers him that he takes her by the hair and throws her into the sea, and she would have drowned had not Hartmut rescued her. Gerlind and her daughter Ortrun have come down to the shore to greet the returning conquerors, but when Gerlind is about to greet Gudrun with a kiss, the angry maiden steps back in disgust, knowing that the haughty queen is to blame for all her misfortune. Hartmut still hopes to win her love and treats her with great kindness; but soon he is compelled to go on an expedition, and Gudrun is at the mercy of the cruel Gerlind, who separates her from her maidens and compels her to go barefoot in the snow and wash clothes in the sea. Only the faithful maid Hildeburg is allowed to share Gudrun's tasks. One day, while they are at work, a swan appears and tells them that they are soon to be rescued. Early next morning, while Gudrun and Hildeburg are again at work on the shore, a boat approaches in which are two men, who prove to be Ortwin and Herwig. They inform Gudrun and Hildeburg that the old heroes Wate, Frute, and Horand are coming with a large army to attack the Normans. Gudrun now defiantly throws the clothes into the sea and proudly returns to the castle. She pretends at last to be willing to marry Hartmut, and a great feast is prepared, and costly garments are provided for her and her maidens.

On the following morning the Hegelingen storm the castle, and a fierce conflict ensues. King Ludwig falls, and Hartmut is saved only by the intercession of his sister Ortrun, who has been kind to Gudrun in her captivity. The Hegelingen take fearful vengeance upon the Normans, but peace is finally made and they return to their home with rich booty and many captives, among them Hartmut and Ortrun. Happy at meeting her daughter again Queen Hilde forgets her hatred of the Normans, and a triple wedding takes place; Gudrun marries Herwig, Ortwin the princess Ortrun, and Hartmut is wedded to Hildeburg.

2. The Epics of Chivalry

From 1170 to 1250 French romances were most popular at the courts. The works of the Trouvères were translated by knight-poets into German. The stories of King Arthur and his Round Table represented ideal knighthood and furnished material for German epics. Heinrich von Veldeke, who makes an exception in selecting the story of Aeneas for his epic, was considered the father of chivalric poetry by his contemporaries. The three most prominent epic poets of the Hohenstaufen are Hartmann von Aue, Gottfried von Strassburg, and Wolfram von Eschenbach.

Hartmann von Aue

As vassal of the lords von Aue, the poet took the name Hartmann von Aue. He took part in the crusade of 1197, and was distinguished for his learning. Besides love songs, he wrote two romances, *Erec* and *Iwein*, and two legends, *Gregorius* and *Der arme Heinrich*. The romances were based upon the Arthur romances, which were taken from the French poet Chrestien de Troyes; *Gregorius* is founded on a French poem, while his best-known work, *Der arme Heinrich*, is taken from a Latin story.

Erec, a knight of the Round Table, has grown careless and indifferent concerning his duties and spends his time in idleness at the side of his wife Enite, neglecting to visit the court. When his wife tries to rouse him from his sloth, he becomes angry and forces her to start out with him to seek for adventures. As a punishment, she is not allowed to speak to him, even when his life is in danger, but, when she repeatedly forgets his commands and her own life is threatened, he rescues her. She has manifested constancy, patience, and humility, which soften him and win his love anew. Reunited they live at Arthur's court until after the death of Erec's father, when Erec ascends the throne.

IWEIN. The knight Iwein is a counterpart of Erec. As the latter forgot his knightly duties by paying too much attention to his wife, Iwein is in danger of neglecting his wife by continued absence from her. He had promised his wife Laudine, when he set out in search of adventures, to return within a year, but breaks his promise and trifles away her affection. Lunete, her servant, appears at King Arthur's court, accuses Iwein of infidelity, and snatches the ring of her mistress from his finger. This drives him to madness and he lives a long time alone in a forest, until three women find him and cure him with a magic salve. He then leaves the forest, taking with him a lion which he has rescued from a dragon, and together they overcome two giants and free three hundred maidens from imprisonment. After gaining fresh renown at Arthur's court as the "Knight with the Lion," Iwein returns to his wife and again wins her love.

GREGORIUS. While a child, Gregory is put into a boat and drifts to a foreign shore. There he is reared by an abbot, who learns from a slate which he finds in the boat that the boy is of a royal family. When he is fifteen years old Gregory discovers the secret of his birth, starts out to find his home, and comes to a country which is being invaded by an enemy. He liberates the queen and marries her, but is horribly shocked when he learns that she is his mother. He immediately leaves her, does penance, and lives miraculously for seventeen years on a lonely island in the sea. Here he is found by the Romans, who inform him that God has ordained him pope. When his mother hears of the miracles which the new pope has wrought on the sick, she, too, makes a pilgrimage to Rome. Here mother and son recognize each other and they live side by side in the pious fulfillment of their duties.

DER ARME HEINRICH. Heinrich von Aue is a rich, handsome

and beloved knight of noble birth, whose home is in Swabia. He is suddenly stricken with leprosy and is avoided by everybody, for no physician is able to heal him. A wise man of Salerno alone knows of a remedy, which, however, seems unattainable; it is the life blood of a young maiden who is willing to die for him. With a sad heart Heinrich returns home, gives away the greater part of his possessions, and lives with a simple farmer who is very much attached to him. The childish and loving presence of the farmer's nine-year old daughter is his only comfort, and when years afterward she learns how the knight may be restored to health, she resolves to sacrifice herself for him. Heinrich and her parents try in vain to dissuade her, but finally allow her to accompany the knight to Salerno. When poor Heinrich hears the physician whetting his knife, a feeling of remorse for his selfishness comes over him, and he forces his way into the master's room and demands that the life of the maiden be spared. He is now resigned to the will of God. This resignation is his salvation, for he soon recovers and returns to Swabia, where the self-sacrificing young maiden becomes his wife.

GOTTFRIED VON STRASSBURG

Gottfried von Strassburg, the author of the famous epic poem *Tristan und Isolde*, was a man of genius, but lacked simplicity and originality. We know very little about his life, but we are told that he died about 1210, before his great work was finished. From the title "Master Gottfried" instead of "Sir Gottfried" we conclude that he was not a knight. His epic, *Tristan und Isolde*, was borrowed from a French poem and represents the irresistible force of love.

TRISTAN UND ISOLDE. After relating the history of Tristan's parents, King Riwalin of Parmenia and his wife Blanchefleur, Gottfried describes the youthful experiences of his hero. Tristan, who when a boy had lost his parents, seeks honor at the court of his uncle, King Marke, in Cornwall, England. In a duel he kills Duke Morold, a relative of the king of Ireland, but receives a wound from his poisoned sword which can not be healed except by the wife of the Irish king. As a gleeman, Tantris by name, he comes to the Irish court, is introduced to the queen, who then heals him, and he finally instructs Isolde, her daughter, in music. He returns to Cornwall and describes the beautiful maiden to his uncle, Marke, who now has a strong desire to possess her, and sends Tristan back to Ireland to woo her for him. At first he succeeds in remaining incognito, but is finally discovered to be Morold's murderer. When Isolde learns this, she attempts to kill him, but her mother intervenes. Tristan, finding that he can not gain his purpose by cunning, informs the queen of his mission, and she succeeds in obtaining the consent of the king to the marriage. Before the party starts for Cornwall, the queen gives to her niece Brangäne, who is to accompany Isolde, a love potion which she is to give to Marke and his bride on their wedding day. On the way, however, Tristan and Isolde unsuspectingly empty the goblets, which they thought filled with wine, and forget that King Marke is awaiting them. Arriving at Cornwall, Isolde is married to the king, but persists in her love for Tristan. When Marke learns of this secret love he compels Tristan to leave the court. As an exile now, he wanders through many lands in search of adventure, until he comes to the duke of Arundel, who also has a daughter by the name of Isolde. Tristan falls in love with her, but can not forget Isolde of Ireland, and often accuses himself of infidelity.

This is the end of Gottfried's poem. Later writers have continued the story, which concludes with the marriage of Tristan with Isolde of Arundel. At death, the two lovers, Tristan and Isolde of Ireland, are reunited and buried in one grave.

WOLFRAM VON ESCHENBACH

Wolfram von Eschenbach, the greatest German poet of the Middle Ages, took his name from the village of Eschenbach, near Ansbach in Bavaria, where he was perhaps born and where he was buried. He was a knight in the service of Count von Wertheim, although he may not have been of noble birth. He owned a little fief, Wildenberg, which was given to him by the count. Again and again he left his home and family to visit at the Wartburg, where he found Landgrave Hermann of Thuringia, who died in 1217, the most appreciative and zealous patron of his art. Wolfram died about 1220. His most celebrated work is *Parzival*. He also wrote two incomplete poems: *Willehalm*, after a French model, and *Titurel*, taken from the saga-cycle of *Parzival*.

PARZIVAL

Parzival was partly borrowed from French poems of Celtic origin, and represents deep religious ideas. Since the poet could neither read nor write, his sources were often misinterpreted. *Parzival* represents knighthood as a powerful moral force in life and teaches that man can only find salvation through faith. Doubt may condemn a man, but manly courage elevates him.

This epic opens with the history of Parzival's father, Gahmuret, the younger son of King Gandin of Anjou, who, not wishing to serve his elder brother, sets out to seek his fortune in the East. He enters the service of the Caliph of Bagdad and wins the hand of the Moorish queen, Belakane, whom he has rescued from her enemies; but, before the birth of their son Feirefiz, Gahmuret's roving spirit urges him on, and he makes the difference of religions a pretext for leaving her. Gahmuret, in the course of his adventures, reaches France and takes part in a tournament; the prize, Herzeloide, Queen of Valois, falls to him, and he marries her. But again he becomes restless, and goes back to the East and falls in battle.

Herzeloide now devotes herself entirely to her son, Parzival. To remove him from the temptations which proved so fatal to his father, she leaves her court and retires into the wilderness of Soltane, where young Parzival grows up in ignorance of the world. When he once hears his mother use the word God, he says: "O tell me, mother, what is God?" She answers: "He is brighter than the day, yet his countenance is as the countenance of men." One day while out hunting, he meets some knights in shining armor; thinking each of them must be a god, he falls on his knees before them. They inform him that they are not gods, but knights, and explain to him what knighthood is. At once a longing to be a knight seizes him, and his mother's entreaties are powerless to turn him from his determination to go to King Arthur's court. She dresses him in fool's garb, in the hope that he may be ridiculed and return to her; but as soon as he is out of sight she dies of a broken heart. Unaware of his mother's death, Parzival journeys on, following in childlike obedience too literally the advice she has given him.

His mother has called him only *bon fils*, *cher fils*, or *beau fils*, and he does not even know his name until he learns it from his mother's niece, Sigune. Parzival arrives at Arthur's court and soon proves himself a dangerous opponent. In ignorance of the laws of chivalry, he slays the Red Knight, Ither, plunders the body, and rides away on Ither's horse to the castle of the old knight Gurnemanz, who becomes his teacher. Among other things Gurnemanz warns him against useless questions.

Parzival again goes forth, still innocent of wrong, but no longer a simpleton, and by his bravery wins the hand of the beautiful queen Condwiramurs of Pelrapeire. They live very happily together; but the desire to see his mother and the love of adventure soon lure him away from his wife. After a day's ride he arrives at a lake, and is invited by a fisherman to lodge at a neighboring castle. Here he is well received and is ushered into a hall, where he sees many strange and beautiful things. Four hundred knights surround the wounded host, who is no other than Anfortas, the King of the Grail. Through a half-open door Parzival sees a beautiful old man lying on a couch. The knights go through the mystic ceremony of the Grail,—Parzival hears on all sides the groans and lamentations as the bleeding spear is borne through the hall; but he remembers the teaching of Gurnemanz, and even when Anfortas alludes to his suffering, Parzival refrains from asking questions. Next morning when Parzival awakes from troubled slumbers he finds the castle deserted, but his horse is at the door. He rides out into the forest until he again meets Sigune, who interprets the wonders through which he has just passed. Parzival has been at Mont Salvat, the home of the Grail-King Anfortas. The simple inquiry of sympathy which was expected from him would have healed the king's wound, and Parzival himself would have become the sovereign of the Grail. Parzival sorrowfully goes his way, and not until he has reached Arthur's camp does he realize the enormity of his offense. He has just been received with honor as a Knight of the Round Table. At the feast which follows, a terrible woman appears,—it is Cundrie, the messenger of the Grail. She curses Parzival for his lack of sympathy. He has forfeited the great prize, is accursed of fortune, unworthy of honor, and beyond the hope of salvation. Laden with such a curse Parzival no longer considers himself worthy of a seat at the Round Table and determines to renounce all pleasure until he has found the Grail anew, and made the inquiry concerning the king's misfortune.

When his friend Gawan wishes him God's blessing on his journey, he calls out: "What is God?" He believes that if there were a divine power it would not have allowed this disgrace to come upon him. He renounces his allegiance to God and declares that God may punish him if it pleases Him. With doubt in his heart Parzival leaves Arthur's court.

To give us a complete picture of chivalrous life, the poet, after describing the deeds of Parzival, introduces Gawan, who represents the worldly elements in contradistinction to Parzival, the representative of the higher life. For five long years Parzival wanders about on land and sea, and the author allows us to see him only at long intervals still seeking the Grail.

On a Good Friday morning he meets a pilgrim knight who directs him to the pious hermit Trevrizent, Parzival's own uncle. Parzival confesses his sins and learns from Trevrizent the mysteries of the Grail.

Again Parzival sallies forth and meets a heathen knight in splendid armor,—it is Feirefiz, his brother. As strangers the two knights engage in a fierce combat. Parzival's spear is broken, but Feirefiz is too magnanimous to take advantage of his opponent's misfortune and asks him his name. Recognition follows, and together they ride to King Arthur, who admits Feirefiz to the Round Table on the following day.

Cundrie once more appears; this time to declare that Parzival has been ordained King of the Grail. Parzival presents himself before Anfortas and asks the important question, and from that moment Anfortas is healed and Parzival is proclaimed king.

3. The Lyric Poetry of the Courts

THE MINNESINGERS. For about two centuries (1150–1350) the literature of Germany was under the influence of the Minnesingers, who were imitators of the French Troubadours. The word "Minnesang" is used to designate the court lyrics in general, because its theme is "Minne" or "Frauendienst" (reverence for womanhood); but some of these songs were also of a religious character, inspired by the crusades. The Minnesinger invented his own form of stanza and his own tune, and was sometimes a wandering peasant who went from village to village singing his songs, or very often an educated singer who practiced his art at the court. The language was the Swabian dialect of the Hohenstaufen.

Tieck thus describes the character of the Minnesang of the Swabian era: "Believers sang of faith; lovers of love; knights described knightly actions and battles; and loving, believing knights were their chief audiences. The spring, beauty, gayety, were subjects that could never tire; great duels and deeds of arms carried away every hearer, the more surely the stronger they were painted; and as the pillars and dome of the church encircled the flock, so did religion, as the highest authority, influence poetry and reality, and every heart in equal love humbled itself before it."

WALTHER VON DER VOGELWEIDE. Walther's songs themselves give us information concerning his life. The date, as well as the locality of his birth and death, is unknown. Tradition has it that he died and lies buried in Würzburg; but several places claim the honor of being his birthplace, among them the modest castle of Vogelweide, in Southern Tyrol. He says in one of his songs: "In Austria I learned to sing," perhaps at the court of the dukes Leopold and Friedrich. We must believe that Walther was a South German, for he used the Bavarian dialect. He may have been of noble family, but he was so poor that he was compelled to wander from court to court, dependent upon the generosity of his patrons. Walther frequently visited at the Court of the Land-grave of Thuringia. When in 1215 the Hohenstaufen Friedrich II. came to the throne, a fief was given to the poet which enabled him to live free from want.

"It is very little," he says in another song, "and of that the priests, who have chests full, come and demand a goodly share."

Walther's poems are distinguished by sincerity and a wide range of thought. He followed the crusades and was a keen observer of the world. Most of his poems are, however, love songs which are pure and highly extol woman's gentle qualities. He oftentimes criticises the conditions of the empire, praises generosity, complains of the instability of worldly things, and admonishes men to self-control and brotherly kindness. An ancient portrait of the poet represents him as he pictures himself in the poem, meditating on honor, worldly good, and God's grace:

> Upon a stone, moss-sheeted,
> Cross-legged I was seated;
> My arms upon my knees did rest.
> Whilst in my hands, as in a nest,
> Both chin and cheeks lay nicely.
> Then pondered I how wisely
> We in this world might move and live,
> Yet could my mind no counsel give.

—Kröger.

Cf. Longfellow's *Walter von der Vogelweid.*

4. DIDACTIC POETRY

During the two centuries following the decline of the Swabian Era, German literature gradually assumed a more practical character. Nevertheless some of the sententious poetry of the Minnesingers, reaching back even to the Spervogel collection in the twelfth century, was didactic, but now the writing of didactic poems was left almost entirely to the clergy and the bourgeois poets. The only nobleman of this time who attempted didactic poetry was HERR VON WINSBACH, a Bavarian, whose work *Der Winsbeke* is superior to the later writings of this period. This poem, which is in the form of a father's counsels to his son, in fifty-six stanzas, expounds and idealizes the system of knighthood.

FREIDANK'S *Bescheidenheit* is the most popular collection of gnomes in the Hohenstaufen period. It consists of epigrammatic poems which admonish men to be virtuous and refined, to treat women respectfully, to live circumspectly and avoid vices of all kinds, and to use good practical common sense.

STRICKER, an Austrian of the middle of the thirteenth century, is recognized as the most prominent German mediaeval story-teller. He was not only an epic poet, but also a satirist, and his tales generally end with a moral.

HUGO VON TRIMBERG lived at the close of the Hohenstaufen period, and is the best representative of didactic poetry after Freidank. His long poem *Renner*, written in his old age, is a sort of code of morals for those who can not understand the writings of the church fathers. In it he preaches against pride, greed, avarice, intemperance, and the higher classes.

THE CLOSE OF THE MIDDLE AGES

With the extinction of the Hohenstaufen the German Empire lost its importance as a united power. It began to be divided into territories whose princes considered their oath of allegiance as a mere formality, while the emperors sought only to establish and enlarge their power. The spirit of chivalry was dying out among the nobles, and gradually new customs and ideas were fostered by the burgher classes, which led to jealousy and civil strife. During the fourteenth and fifteenth centuries no poetical work of any value was produced, but the people were rapidly rising in intelligence and culture. German industry, discoveries, the arts of engraving, woodcarving, and printing flourished. Great cathedrals were building, and universities were established, while the expansive power of Germany in relation to other countries was on the decline.

There were still wandering minstrels, but they had become very inferior and devoted themselves to the Volkslied, which was often crude and without beauty. Two noblemen, GRAF VON MONTFORT and OSWALD VON WOLKENSTEIN, as well as the poet HEINRICH VON MEISSEN, called "Frauenlob," strove, it is true, to preserve the spirit of chivalry and the Minnesang, but without success.

When the Minnesingers had passed away, another class of poets, the MEISTERSINGERS, attempted

to carry on the work in a more scholarly and systematic manner. Many of the old Minnesingers were
called Masters; in fact they were the founders of
the Meistergesang, which reached its highest development in the sixteenth century, when guilds and
singing schools had been established in Ulm, Augsburg, Nuremberg, and many other cities. The members of these guilds were required to observe good
morals and lead an honorable life. The aspirant
for honors in one of these schools had to pass through
four preliminary grades; he first learned, as "Schü-
ler," the laws of the "Tabulatur." These learned,
he became a "Schulfreund," and when he had mas-
tered at least four tunes he was called a "Singer."
The rank of "Dichter" was attained by the composition of a new text, while the highest honor, "Meister,"
was conferred only on a poet who had invented a
new tune. The "Sängerkrieg" at the Wartburg,
which dates back to the close of the thirteenth century, gives a good illustration of the Singing Contest, which later played a very important part in
the schools of the Meistersingers. One singer chal-
lenged another and the "Merker" decided on their
respective merits. The greatest of the Meistersingers was Hans Sachs, the "cobbler bard" of Nuremberg.

The German VOLKSLIED, which had existed from
the earliest times, was, according to Herder, "the
voice of the whole nation." We find in these songs

much that was popular in the Minnesang:—nature, domestic infelicity, love, feasts, and dancing. Although they were often faulty and inartistic, they were nevertheless fresh and true to life. Religious topics, also, had at all times filled an important place in the Volkslied. The historical ballad reached its highest development in the two centuries immediately preceding the Reformation. At this time appeared many of those songs which Herder, Brentano, von Arnim, and finally Uhland collected, and which live on among the German people to-day. Among them some good hunting and drinking songs may be found, also some excellent ballads like *Heidenröslein*, which have been recast by the great poets of the nineteenth century, and have thus become the property of the people.

About the fifteenth century the verse epic was supplanted by the prose romance borrowed from Latin, French, and Italian sources. Many of these stories, like the pranks of TILL EULENSPIEGEL, were published in the form of *Volksbücher*, which became very popular, and are still read.

The Beast Epic *Reineke Fuchs*, however, continued to assert its place in German literature. This translation of the Low German poem *Reynke de Vos* was published at Lübeck in 1498, and has, as Carlyle says, "extinguished all the rest, inasmuch as all subsequent translations and editions have derived themselves from it." Goethe's version of it has made it continue as one of the most popular German books ever written.

The most important work at the close of the Middle Ages is SEBASTIAN BRANT'S *Narrenschiff*, which reveals many follies of the age and describes various kinds of fools on their way to "Narragonien" (Fool's land). It was translated into Latin, English, Dutch, and French.

The DRAMA had its origin among the early Teutons and was fostered and cultivated by the church and the clergy. From the Latin Christmas and Easter plays, which may be traced back to the Carlovingian period, there gradually developed a German religious drama. Material for these dramas was found in the Mysteries and Passion Plays, the story of the Wise and the Foolish Virgins, the Virgin Mary, and the various saints. The Oberammergau Passion Play, which is performed at the little village of Oberammergau in Bavaria every ten years, is a relic of these ancient Mysteries. The *Fastnachtsspiel* (Carnival Play) was especially popular during the fifteenth century, and marks the rise of the secular drama. On Shrove Tuesday the young people in the towns presented dramatic scenes representing the clownish peasant, the quarrelsome wife, the quack doctor, the beggar-monk, or the dissolute prince or king. It remained for Hans Sachs to make these farces of lasting interest and value.

THE PERIOD OF THE RENAISSANCE AND THE REFORMATION

HUMANISM and the Renaissance, inventions and discoveries, all united to revolutionize the world at the close of the fifteenth century. The Humanistic movement, an intellectual revolution, was a test of reason as applied to the ethics of conduct. The Humanists were the pioneers of the Renaissance in Germany and helped prepare the way for the Reformation. The German Renaissance, which was a revival not only of the spirit of classic antiquity but also of its forms, vitalized the Humanists, and during the Reformation was confined almost exclusively to the religious life. The establishment of universities, the revival of classical learning, the invention of printing, and the discovery of America contributed largely to change the intellectual movement in German literature. The Reformation, too, enlisted all powers to produce a new epoch in German history and literature at the beginning of the sixteenth century. Carlyle in describing this period says: "At the era of the Reformation the didactic spirit reaches its acme." Political and religious freedom, as well as ecclesiastical controversies, occupied the writers of both prose and poetry. Much was expected from the new struggles for liberty and the Protestant cause, but at the close of the century fanaticism, dissensions, and the decline of this new literature were manifest. Luther was not spared by his enemies, among whom we may mention the Franciscan monk THOMAS MURNER of Strassburg; nor did he lack stanch supporters like ULRICH VON HUTTEN. Many of the church hymns which were written at this time give evidence of religious struggles; but about 1530, satires, fables, anecdotes, and dramatic productions show a tendency to ridicule, teach, and amuse. Besides the *Volkslied*, which also flourished in this period, the so-called *Volksbücher* retained their popularity. They consisted in part of sagas which were applied to certain persons like the magician *Johann Faust* and *Der Ewige Jude;* in part, of satires like the adventures of the *Schildbürger*.

The principal representatives of the Reformation period in German literature besides Martin Luther are Hans Sachs and Johann Fischart.

MARTIN LUTHER (November 10, 1483–February 18, 1546) was born at Eisleben and educated at Magdeburg, Eisenach, and Erfurt. He first intended to study law, but, frightened by a thunderstorm, decided to become a monk, and lived in the monastery at Erfurt from 1505 to 1508, when he was appointed professor of philosophy at the University of Wittenberg. In 1511 he spent four weeks in Rome, where he was surprised and shocked by the worldliness of the pope and the immorality and irreligion of the clergy.

After receiving the degree of doctor of theology at the University of Wittenberg in 1512, he lectured there on the Scriptures and preached at the Augustinian monastery at Erfurt. On October 31, 1517, he nailed the ninety-five theses, opposing the sale of indulgences, on the church door in Wittenberg. Then followed his disputation with Dr. Eck at Leipzig in June, 1519, and his excommunication in 1520. In December of this same year he burned the papal bull with the papal decretals before the Elster gate in the presence of students and professors. Summoned to Worms in January of the next year to answer for his conduct, he defended his faith in God and the Bible and refused to recant. On his return from Worms he found a safe refuge with the Elector Friedrich, at the Wartburg, where, as "Junker Jörg," he began his translation of the Bible. Returning to Wittenberg, he threw his whole strength into the work of the Reformation, of which he was the central figure. In 1525 he married Katharina von Bora, a former nun. He spent the next twenty years of his life in Wittenberg, but his death occurred while he was on a visit to Eisleben, his birthplace. Luther's translation of the Scriptures, the last edition of which was published in 1545, was of the greatest importance, because it was free from localisms and could be easily

understood by all. Luther and Philip Melanchthon,
we are told, once disputed over a certain passage:—
" All I care for," said Melanchthon " is the Greek,"
" And all I care for," answered Luther, "is the German."   Besides his translations, Luther was the author of many sermons, table talks, and evangelical hymns. The first German hymnal appeared in
1524.   In all, thirty-seven hymns are ascribed to
Luther, among them the well-known hymn *Ein' feste
Burg ist unser Gott.* While attending the Imperial
Diet at Augsburg in 1530, he translated thirteen of
Aesop's fables into German. A collection of 2900 letters, some in Latin, the majority in German, are addressed to the pope, princes, and clergy, and to friends
and members of his family. While Luther lived he
was the main vital religious force in Germany, the
center of enthusiasm and educational influence; when
he died the unity of German Protestantism died with
him.

HANS SACHS (1494–1576), one of the most loyal
supporters of Luther and the Reformation, was born
at Nuremberg. His father was a tailor, but Hans,
who attended school until fifteen years of age, was
apprenticed to a shoemaker. After five years of
extensive travel in Germany and Tyrol, visiting the
various schools of the Meistersingers, he returned to
his native city, where he died in 1576. Hans Sachs
was a great poet. His powers of description, his fund
of humor, his clear style, and the great variety of

subjects treated, made him the most popular poet
of the sixteenth century. He wrote more than 6000
pieces of verse,—about 4275 of which are Master-
songs; the rest are dramas, fables, comic stories,
and dialogues. He reformed the Meistergesang, for
which he used biblical material, and was rightly
called the last and best of the Meistersingers.

In his Shrovetide plays more than in any of his
other works he reflected the customs and conditions
of his time, giving us a vivid picture of the beggar-
monk, peasant, merchant, physician, and wandering
gypsy, as well as of married life, which was his
favorite theme. Some of his dramas still live on and
are played by the peasants in Upper Bavaria and
Hungary.

JOHANN FISCHART (about 1550–90), was to his
age, as satirist and story-teller, what Hans Sachs was
as a humorist. He was a native of Alsace, but we
know very little of his life. After visiting England,
France, Flanders, and Italy he lived in Strassburg as
a lawyer, and died in 1589. His command of language was wonderful, his satirical humor well directed, his attacks on the Jesuits being especially
scathing. His style reminds us of Rabelais, whom
he imitated in his *Gargantua*. As a poet we see
him to the best advantage in *Das glückhaft Schiff
von Zürich*. This tells how in the summer of 1576 a
number of Zürich citizens, whom the city of Strassburg had invited to a shooting festival, undertook

to cover the distance by way of the Limmat, Aare, and Rhine in one day. To convince their hosts that this had really been accomplished, they placed before them, when they entered Strassburg in the evening, a large pot of porridge, still hot, which had been cooked before setting out from Zürich in the morning.

THE PERIOD OF THE THIRTY YEARS'
WAR (1618–1712)

IN the latter part of the preceding period literature as well as science was gradually developing; English comedians visited Germany, bringing with them some of Shakespeare's plays and Marlowe's *Faustus;* but progress in all departments of education, culture, and religion was greatly retarded by the terrible conflicts of the Thirty Years' War (1618–48). This struggle between Protestants and Catholics not only devastated and depopulated Germany, but also introduced undesirable foreign customs and threatened a complete dismemberment of the nation. Although the war resulted in the establishment of equal rights for the Catholic, Evangelical, and Reformed churches, the religious life of the people was greatly affected by the bitter strife.

Not until the close of the seventeenth century did Philipp Jakob Spener succeed in inculcating the idea that true piety consists, not in the letter of the law, but in deep religious feeling. Rationalism, which had spread from England and France, found its chief exponent in Leibnitz. The church hymn was the true expression of the religious feeling of the people and found its greatest development in this period.

Scholars and nobles united in an effort to purify the language, and to cultivate a new German literature. To this end the "Fruchtbringende Gesellschaft" or "Palmenorden" was founded at Weimar in 1617, with the object of purifying the language from foreign words and dialects. It also helped to abolish the coarse tendencies of the sixteenth century, and encouraged artistic expression in both prose and poetry. This society was modeled on the Florentine "Accademia della Crusca," and included princes, nobles, and scholars, regardless of their religious beliefs. Similar societies were formed in other places, the most famous of which was the "Gesellschaft der Schäfer an der Pegnitz" in Nuremberg. While the results of these literary societies were unimportant, they may have helped in some measure towards the solid foundation of modern literature.

MARTIN OPITZ (1597–1639) sought in quite a different manner to reform German literature by imitating the Greeks and Romans. His *Buch von der deutschen Poeterey* (1624) was considered the chief authority on versification, composition, and style until Gottsched's *Critische Dichtkunst* appeared. He wrote some excellent poems, and some of his hymns were included in the church hymnal, but in the novel and drama he never got beyond translation, for, although he possessed a versatile talent, he was not a creative genius. Opitz was born at Bunzlau in Silesia, and was the founder of the FIRST SILESIAN SCHOOL OF POETRY. This school strove after purity of diction and simplicity of style, but became too artificial to be of lasting influence.

Among the followers of Opitz are SIMON DACH, the center of a poetic society in Königsberg, and author of the popular Volkslied *Ännchen von Tharau;* PAUL FLEMING, a young poet of great promise who died in his thirty-first year; also FRIEDRICH LOGAU, a writer of epigrams.

ANDREAS GRYPHIUS (1616–64), the last representative of this school, was not only considered an able writer of lyric poetry, but was also a recognized authority among dramatists. It is strange that this man of melancholy temperament, who delighted in ghost scenes and reveled in carnage, should have succeeded better as a writer of comedies than of tragedies. His naïve humor is best seen in his *Horribilicribrifax*, which satirizes the military ostentation of the times. Gryphius imitated Shakespeare's *Midsummer Night's Dream* in his comedy *Peter Squenz*, a witty burlesque on the dramatic ignorance of the Meistersingers. Notwithstanding his faults and stilted style, Gryphius succeeded in appealing to the imagination of his readers and making even the driest subjects interesting. He forms, as it were, the connecting link between the first and second Silesian schools.

The efforts of the first Silesian school to create a pure style soon degenerated into the bombast of the SECOND SILESIAN SCHOOL, which rose into existence under the leadership of two noblemen, HOFFMANSWALDAU and LOHENSTEIN. These men were deficient in original genius, and simply imitated and exaggerated the characteristics of Opitz and Gryphius, which aroused such a disgust that a reaction was inevitable. One of the chief reactionaries was CHRISTIAN WEISSE, rector of the Gymnasium at Zittau, who, as a good German pedagogue, stood for the purity and simplicity of the German language. He was a prolific writer of school dramas, which were mostly didactic, and were presented by his pupils. Weisse was strong in presenting contrasts, and delighted in surprises, but his dramas do not read well, because he introduced too many characters. Two other opponents of the second Silesian school were HEINRICH BROCKES and CHRISTIAN GÜNTHER. The former fell under the influence of English writers, was a great lover of nature and a religious enthusiast. His poetry was collected under the title *Irdisches Vergnügen in Gott*. Günther was a genuine genius, but his wild and dissolute habits brought him to an early grave. In his best hours he was very religious, and his songs of love, sorrow, and repentance undoubtedly express his own feelings, but they are sometimes marred by coarseness.

In the second half of the seventeenth century satire

became a subordinate element in the German novel. French and Spanish models prevailed. The greatest novel of this period is *Simplicissimus*. The author of this work, CHRISTOFFEL VON GRIMMELSHAUSEN, had, as a boy, passed through the horrors and vicissitudes of the Thirty Years' War. This novel, which incorporates many of his own experiences, is written in firm prose and gives a realistic picture of the demoralized condition of Germany at this time. In many respects it may be considered a counterpart to *Parzival*. Another writer of this class who was influenced by Spanish models is HANS MOSCHEROSCH. His chief work is a satirical romance, *Wunderliche und wahrhafte Gesichte Philanders von Sittewald*, in which, in the form of visions, he depicts from his own experience the misery and oppression of his humiliated fatherland.

The most important foreign imitations of this period are the *Robinsonaden*, modeled on Defoe's *Robinson Crusoe*, which is an expression of the spirit of adventure foreshadowed in *Simplicissimus*. It was at once translated into German, and imitations representing every country, and almost every trade, sprung up all over Germany; among these, *Insel Felsenberg*, by J. G. SCHNABEL, is the best.

As a conclusion to the period of the Thirty Years' War we may call attention to the influence of ABRAHAM A SANTA CLARA, a court-preacher in Vienna. His homilies and didactic writings are distinguished by brilliant wit and scathing remarks concerning the customs of the times. *Judas der Erzschelm* is his best work. Schiller found his material for the sermon of the Capuchin monk in *Wallensteins Lager* in a volume of Santa Clara's tractates.

Among the best known hymn writers of this period are: JOHANN SCHEFFLER, who wrote a collection of hymns called *Heilige Seelenlust;* FRIEDRICH VON SPEE, a Jesuit, whose hymns were published under the title *Trutz-Nachtigal;* JOACHIM NEANDER, author of the well-known hymn *Lobe den Herren den mächtigen König der Ehren;* PAUL GERHARDT, the most celebrated of all, who wrote 131 sacred songs, some of which are very beautiful, as *Nun ruhen alle Wälder; Wie soll ich dich empfangen?* and *Befiehl du deine Wege;* and GRAF VON ZINZENDORF, founder of the Moravian Brotherhood of Herrnhut.

THE PERIOD OF FREDERICK THE GREAT
(1712–86)

AT the close of the seventeenth century Germany had not yet fully recovered from the effects of the Thirty Years' War. France and England had surpassed Germany in intellectual activity, but now a new life began to manifest itself. Rationalism and then individualism developed with remarkable rapidity and Germany soon rivaled the other nations of Europe in philosophy and literature. Frederick the Great, who disdained to read the productions of the German poets, has left us a number of poems, letters, and political and historical works, all written in French, and yet he exerted a powerful influence on the development of German literature. His great deeds, which again gave to the Germans a hero, awakened patriotic life; his own literary activity stimulated his contemporaries, and even his aversion to German poetry was an incentive to German writers to put French literature to the test and produce something better.

Prominent as forerunners of the classical period we must mention GOTTSCHED and BODMER. The history of our modern German classical period began with a literary controversy between Gottsched and

his Leipzig friends on the one side, and Bodmer and
BREITINGER, who were representatives of the Swiss
party, on the other. In the first part of the eighteenth
century Leipzig and Zürich were the chief centers
of literary activity. Gottsched, who was a professor
at the University of Leipzig, claimed that it was
necessary for a poet to follow certain theoretical rules.
He imitated French models, emphasized moral principles in literature, and tried to reform the German
stage by the introduction of the French classical
drama. Bodmer and Breitinger did not object to
rules, but sought rather to reform literature by
placing greater stress upon the nature of poetic cre-
ation; upon the feeling and fancy of the poet and the
impression made on the reader. They took the
Greeks and English as models, especially Homer and
Milton. Gottsched gradually lost his friends, and
the rapidly advancing spirit of the age declared him
defeated.

ALBRECHT VON HALLER, a physician in Bern, and
FRIEDRICH VON HAGEDORN in Hamburg, although
poets of independent standpoint, ably supported the
ideas and theories advanced by Bodmer. Haller
obtained recognition through his *Oden* and his
masterly description of nature in his poem *Die Alpen.*
Hagedorn was a poet of a lighter vein and introduced
the Anacreontic style of poetry into German literature. He was the author of *Oden und Lieder, Fabeln und Erzählungen,* and a contributor to various

literary periodicals. A company of younger poets, who became disgusted with Gottsched's pedantry, founded a new literary journal known as the *Bremer Beiträge*. Among the contributors were some of the best writers of the time, as Gellert, Elias Schlegel, Zachariä, Rabener, and Klopstock.

CHRISTIAN GELLERT was, next to Klopstock, the most prominent contributor to the *Beiträge*, and also the most popular of the Leipzig writers. As professor of philosophy at the University of Leipzig he was deeply beloved, and Goethe, who was at one time his pupil, says that his lecture room was always crowded. His *Fabeln* were appreciated by all classes alike, and his spiritual hymns are to be found in our German hymnals to-day. His *Erzählungen* are characterized by their simplicity and naïveté.

One of the master minds of this period was JOHANN WINCKELMANN, who, by his *Geschichte der Kunst des Alterthums*, aroused the German people to a new appreciation of art and greatly influenced Lessing and Goethe. About the middle of the eighteenth century, Halle and Berlin strove to become the great literary centers of Germany, but towards the close of the century Weimar succeeded in attracting the attention of the whole educated world. Gleim, Uz, and Götz, students at the University of Halle, founded the Anacreontic School of poetry about 1740. "Vater Gleim" became popular through his patriotic songs and his enthusiasm for

Frederick the Great. He was the leader of this school and did much to encourage the younger poets of the day. In Berlin, KARL W. RAMLER, through his odes and Horatian love poetry, became the acknowledged representative of poetic style. Among the most prominent of all the patriotic poets of the period was EWALD C. VON KLEIST, an officer in the Prussian army, who was mortally wounded in the battle of Kunersdorf, in 1759. Encouraged by Gleim, Kleist devoted his talents to poetry and became the intimate friend of Lessing. He was an ardent lover of nature, as is evinced in his poem *Der Frühling* (1749).

FRIEDRICH GOTTLIEB KLOPSTOCK (1724–1803)

Klopstock may well be considered the reformer of German literature. He brought order out of chaos, studied Milton and the classics, and claimed that rhyme was unnecessary, that fancy and a pleasing style were the real essentials of poetry. Although Klopstock enjoyed a long life, nearly eighty years, his literary development was of short duration, for at twenty-four he had reached the height of his fame. The first three cantos of the *Messias* and his *Odes* are his best productions, and reveal that strong religious idealism which continued to live on in the Protestantism of the time. Klopstock was born at Quedlinburg in 1724. He attended the celebrated classical school at Schulpforta, where his literary tastes began to develop, and then studied at Jena and

Leipzig. While a tutor at Langensalza in 1750, he was invited by Bodmer, a friend of his father, who had become interested in his *Messias*, to visit him in Zürich. He remained only six months with Bodmer, whose displeasure he aroused by his lack of application to the great work, and was glad to accept an offer from the king of Denmark, Frederick V., to make Copenhagen his home and complete his work there. On the way he stopped at Hamburg, where he made the acquaintance of Meta Moller, who afterwards became his wife. Although he lived twenty years (1751–1771) in Copenhagen free from all care as to his livelihood, the *Messias* was not finished until 1773. In 1771 he retired to Hamburg, spending the rest of his life there. He died in 1803, and lies buried in Ottensen, near Hamburg. Klopstock's literary activity was not limited to religious writings and the *Odes*. He wished by example and precept to reform the content and form of German poetry. His subject-matter was to be national in scope; he addressed himself to the whole nation, sought his material in the past, and celebrated Arminius, the chief of the Cherusci, in three dramas, the so-called *Bardiete: Hermanns Schlacht, Hermann und die Fürsten*, and *Hermanns Tod*. Klopstock's patriotism found expression also in a "War Song," written in honor of Frederick the Great, but later dedicated to Henry the Fowler.

Like Schiller, he was an ardent advocate of liberty, and rejoiced at the success of the American Revolu-

tion. His strong religious nature is revealed in his
sacred lyrics, which are full of sympathy, feeling, and
earnestness. In the *Messias* we find epic, lyric, and
dramatic elements well combined. It consists of
twenty long cantos, nineteen of which are written
in hexameter verse. Although Klopstock was indebted to Milton's *Paradise Lost* for many descriptions of man's fall and redemption, yet, in spite
of the numerous criticisms of his great work, it
marked the beginning of a new literature for Germany. The poem begins with the scene on the
Mount of Olives and ends with the completion of
man's redemption, when the Savior takes His place
on the throne at the right hand of His Father.

Christoph Martin Wieland (1733–1813)

Wieland is primarily an epic poet, although he produced various kinds of poetry. To a powerful imagination, he, like Klopstock, united that easy, pleasing
style of expression which was so much admired in the
French writings of the day. By this means he succeeded in arousing an interest in German poetry in
those circles where French literature was known and
favored. Although Wieland's works are little read
at the present time, they nevertheless give evidence
of a strong, romantic, and enthusiastic spirit.

In contrast with Klopstock, Wieland's poetic activity underwent many changes; but in every period of
his life he manifested great literary prolificness, so

that long before his death his works were published
in forty-two volumes.

Wieland was born in the little village of Oberholz-
heim near Biberach in Württemberg, where his
father was a Lutheran clergyman. While yet a
student at the University of Tübingen he wrote
several poems, taking Klopstock as his model. Bodmer, the Swiss critic, having read several of these
poems, invited Wieland to Zürich. Here he remained
about seven years as guest and tutor, and then went
to Bern as teacher, returning in 1760 to Biberach,
where he was appointed to an office in the city government. Up to this time Wieland had composed epics,
two dramas, and many hymns, all in the spirit of
Klopstock, although he began even at this time to
clothe his characters in Greek garb. Contemporaneously with his change of residence, Wieland became
less enthusiastic and more frivolous, and vied with
Voltaire in writing satirical and humorous tales.
The most important work written at Biberach, besides translations from Shakespeare, is *Agathon*, a
romance which abounds in long philosophical discussions of moral principles. In 1769 he was called
to the University of Erfurt as Professor of Philosophy,
and in 1772 to Weimar as Hofrat and tutor of Karl
August and Constantine, sons of the Duchess Amalie
where he had the best opportunities for literary work.
He published a magazine, *Der Teutsche Merkur*, devoted to literature and politics, translated Latin and

Greek classics, wrote the operetta *Alceste*, a few romances like *Die Abderiten*, and the most famous of all his works, *Oberon*. This romantic poem is composed of twelve cantos. The material for it was taken from a French romance which tells of the adventures of Huon de Bordeaux, and is skillfully interwoven with the story of the quarrel of Oberon, the king of the elves, with his wife, Titania, as it is given in Shakespeare's *Midsummer Night's Dream*.

The last ten years of his life Wieland spent in Weimar. He died in 1813, and was buried in the garden of his farm at Osmannstedt near Weimar.

Gotthold Ephraim Lessing (1729–81)

Lessing became distinguished in German literature not only as the creator of the German drama, but also as the chief representative of standard prose and religious tolerance. Lessing's life is a story of deprivation and disappointment. He was the oldest of a family of twelve children and was early thrown upon his own resources, since his father was the impecunious pastor of the small church in Kamenz, Saxony. By means of free scholarships he pursued his studies at the Classical School in Meissen, and when seventeen attended the University of Leipzig, where he was to study theology; but he became more interested in literature and the theater. Through the influence of the playwriter Mylius he made the acquaintance of actors and wrote the comedy *Der junge Gelehrte*, which was presented in 1748 by the famous troupe of Frau Neuber. This same year Lessing followed Mylius to Berlin, where he remained until the autumn of 1755, with the exception of one year spent at Wittenberg. Influential friends in Berlin to a great extent directed his activity. His command of the French language brought him into touch with Voltaire whose favor he lost, however, through carelessness and indifference. Of more importance was his friendship with Voss, publisher of the *Vossische Zeitung*, for which he wrote poems and reviews. Lessing became intimate also with the philosopher Moses Mendelssohn and the publisher Nicolai. In the years 1753–55 the young poet and critic published works, which consisted of poems, odes, fables, tales, and the tragedy *Miss Sara Sampson*.

Miss Sara Sampson

This is a domestic tragedy written in prose. Lessing found his material in Richardson's celebrated English romance *Clarissa Harlowe*, and developed it while in Potsdam in 1755. It was presented for the first time at Frankfort-on-the-Oder and was well received. The scene interchanges between two inns of an English town.

ACT I. Mellefont, a weak rather than licentious man, has deserted the passionate and revengeful Marwood, his former mistress, and has abducted the sentimental Sara Sampson, who begs her lover to marry her immediately. But Mellefont can not endure the thought of being bound for a lifetime to one woman, and offers various excuses for postponing the marriage. He learns that Marwood is stopping at a neighboring inn and wishes to speak with him.

Act II. Marwood's attempt to estrange him from Sara only serves to make him love her the more, and he declares that he will marry Sara, even when Marwood tries to intimidate him by drawing a dagger in order to kill him. At the same time he reveals his weakness in that he can not refuse the angry woman's request to see Sara before she leaves the hotel.

Act III. He introduces Marwood as a distant relative, and she tries to gain Sara's sympathy and turn her against her lover. But Sara informs her that every obstacle which might hinder the marriage has been put aside, for her father, Sir William Sampson, whom Marwood has told where the fugitives are hiding, has arrived and forgiven his daughter, and consented to the marriage.

Act IV. Under the pretext of bidding Sara farewell, Marwood again visits her, and craftily induces Mellefont to leave the hotel. When Sara learns who her visitor is she is very much frightened and hastens into her room, where she becomes unconscious. While her maid rushes to her assistance, Marwood, feigning sympathy, also enters, and unnoticed exchanges the medicine for a poisonous powder, which the maid then gives to her mistress.

Act V. Sara feels the approach of death, and Mellefont, who has returned, learns what has taken place. When he realizes that his sweetheart can not recover he resolves to die with her. Both Sara and her father, who is at her bedside, pardon him, whereupon Mellefont stabs himself with the dagger which he has wrested from Marwood.

Lessing's desire to be connected with a theater took him again to Leipzig in the autumn of 1755, but, before he had accomplished much in a literary way, he started on a journey to England with the son of a rich citizen of Leipzig. They had just reached Amsterdam when the outbreak of the Seven Years' War

compelled his companion to return. The occupation
of Leipzig by the Prussians brought Lessing into close
relation with Kleist. When the latter left the city,
Lessing returned to Berlin, where he wrote fables,
critical essays, and a one-act martial drama, *Philotas*.
His friends had meanwhile found him a position as
secretary to General von Tauentzien, whom Frederick
the Great had appointed governor of Silesia, and
whom he now accompanied to Breslau. Here he
lived until 1765, devoting his time to the theater and
to his *Minna von Barnhelm* and *Laokoon*, which were
completed later. Finding his secretaryship burdensome, he returned to Berlin, where he sought the
office of librarian in the royal library, but the king
preferred a Frenchman. In 1767 a German National
Theater was established in Hamburg, and Lessing
accepted the appointment of critic and adviser. The
enterprise was a failure, but to Lessing's connection
with it we owe that masterpiece of criticism, the
Hamburgische Dramaturgie. After leaving Hamburg, in 1770, Lessing was appointed librarian at
Wolfenbüttel where he remained the rest of his life.

*Laokoon, oder über die Grenzen der Malerei und
Poesie*, Lessing's most important prose work, appeared in 1766. It is a critical investigation of the
principles of plastic and poetic art, and was suggested
by a statement in Winckelmann's *Geschichte der
Kunst des Alterthums*. Lessing defines the limitations of the arts, and taking for example the death of

Laokoon shows how differently the poet Virgil and the unknown sculptor treat the same subject. While *Laokoon* is not, strictly speaking, a contradiction of Winckelmann's work, it introduced a new principle into aesthetics, cleared up the confusion which existed regarding the laws of poetry and plastic art, and shows Lessing's unrivaled ability as a critic.

Minna von Barnhelm

Minna von Barnhelm is a five-act comedy which appeared in 1767, and was presented for the first time in the same year in Hamburg. It gives us a vivid picture of the time of the Seven Years' War, and is the first comedy which depicts German customs and German character.

ACT I. As in *Miss Sara Sampson*, so here the scene is laid in a hotel, this time in Berlin. The leading character in the first act is Major von Tellheim, a discharged officer who has been wounded in his right arm. He paid out of his own pocket a deficiency in the war tax in Saxony which he should have collected. After peace had been declared the money was not returned to him, because his integrity was questioned by the government, which believed that he had been bribed by the enemy to pay the deficiency. While waiting for some disposition of his case at the capital his means are exhausted and he can not pay his hotel bills regularly. He feels compelled to dismiss his servant Just, and pawns his engagement ring to pay his bills. Notwithstanding his poverty, he not only refuses to accept the payment of a loan from the widow of his comrade Marloff, but even denies her indebtedness to him. The proffered aid of his former sergeant major Werner is also indignantly rejected.

ACT II. Minna von Barnhelm, an heiress and Tellheim's

fiancée, who has only once heard from him since peace was made, travels to Prussia in search of him. She unwittingly stops at the same hotel in which Major Tellheim has taken up his quarters, and soon learns from the landlord that the major is in straightened circumstances. He shows her the ring, which she immediately recognizes and redeems. She requests an interview with Tellheim without revealing her identity. In the conversation which follows he declares that his misfortune will not permit him to marry her.

ACT III. To vindicate this step he writes Minna a letter in which he minutely gives the reasons for his action. After Minna has read the letter she sends it back to Tellheim by Franziska, her maid, and asks for another interview. Franziska's meeting with Werner introduces a minor episode which takes up the greater part of the third act.

ACT IV. Minna learns through the Frenchman Riccaut that Tellheim's case has taken a successful turn, but this is now a matter of indifference to her. She craftily plans to convert him from his false ideas of honor, and for this purpose instructs Franziska to inform the Major that because of her engagement to him she has been disinherited by her uncle.

ACT V. When Tellheim hears this he is a changed man and believes he is under obligation to share her misfortune. He secures money from Werner to redeem his ring and implores Minna to forget what he has said concerning their marriage. When he is fully exonerated from all blame and reinstated by the king he sees no obstacle in his way; but Minna now uses his own words in proving to him how ignoble it would be for her to allow him to marry one who has been disinherited. Tellheim does not understand the jest even after Just tells him that Minna has redeemed his ring. The arrival of von Bruchsal, her uncle, however, brings about the desired end. The love episode of Werner and Franziska develops into a second marriage.

EMILIA GALOTTI

Lessing transfers the scene of his next tragedy, *Emilia Galotti,* to the duchy of Guastalla on the Po in Italy. Of all Lessing's dramas, this one, which received its present form while Lessing was librarian at Wolfenbüttel in 1772, has the most dramatic action and the best delineated characters. It is a denunciation of the arbitrary power of princes, and like *Miss Sara Sampson* is the story of an abduction.

Act I.   In this act we are introduced to Hettore Gonzaga, the prince of Guastalla, a weak, despotic ruler, concerned only with the gratification of his own personal desires; also to his chamberlain Marinelli, an unprincipled courtier and cunning intriguer, who maintains his influence with the prince by aiding him in his sinful indulgences.   The prince is so captivated by the beauty of a young maiden, Emilia Galotti, that he forgets his former love, Orsina, and neglects his official duties.   When he learns that Emilia is to be married to Count Appiani he is beside himself and calls Marinelli to his aid.   This evil adviser soon conceives a plan; Emilia's lover must be sent out of the city on an embassy without delay, and if this can not be accomplished, force must be used.

Act II.   Emilia's father, Colonel Odoardo Galotti, a man of firm principles, but of passionate temperament, has come from his estate where the wedding is to take place, to learn of the arrangements which his wife has made.   He is displeased when he hears that his daughter has attended mass alone, and becomes very angry when his wife tells him that the prince has been paying attention to Emilia at social affairs.   The father departs and Emilia soon comes into the room; she has inherited her mother's excitable nature and the resolute disposition of her father, and in great distraction tells how the prince sat behind her at mass and accosted her as she was leaving the church.   At the advice of her mother she keeps this a secret, and calmly receives Appiani.   From his brief conversation with Marinelli we are convinced that Appiani is a strong, upright character.   The chamberlain now appears with the request that the count shall leave the city immediately as the ambassador of the prince.   But Appiani, who, at any other time, would feel honored with this commission, refuses to have his marriage postponed, and when Marinelli insults him he challenges him to a duel; the chamberlain leaves with the words, "Be patient; Count, only be patient!"

ACT III. The carriage which is to take the bridal couple and Emilia's mother to the country estate is attacked by men hired for this purpose. A servant of Marinelli, who pretends to come to the rescue of the wedding party, takes Emilia from the carriage to the castle of the prince. Emilia's mother is also taken there, but in the melée Count Appiani is shot; his last word is, "Marinelli."

ACT IV. The abductors have in their plans forgotten two important persons, Orsina and Odoardo Galotti. The former comes unexpectedly to the castle for a final interview, which is refused her. She learns who the guests at the castle are, and, having met on the way the corpse of Appiani, she now sees clearly through the whole sad affair. As she leaves the castle she informs Marinelli of her intention to announce next day on the market place that he is the murderer. Orsina meets Emilia's father at the door, and while Marinelli goes to announce his arrival, Orsina improves the opportunity to inform the colonel of the death of Appiani and of the conversation which Emilia had with the prince at the church. Odoardo becomes fearfully incensed at this, looks about for a weapon and secures a dagger from Orsina. He does not yet know for what purpose he will use it; in any case he wishes his wife to be far away, and therefore begs Orsina to take her with her to the city.

ACT V. Meanwhile Marinelli has planned how Emilia can be permanently separated from her parents. When Odoardo expresses the wish to take his daughter with him, the chamberlain declares in the presence of the prince that the death of Appiani demands an investigation, and it is therefore necessary that father, mother, and daughter be separated. The thought that he is to leave his daughter in the hands of her abductor arouses the father to a terrible deed. He apparently acquiesces in the prince's procedure, and begs only for a brief private interview with Emilia. This request can not be denied him. From the lips of her father Emilia now hears what has happened, and what is impending. She is not terrified by force, but is conscious of her own weakness and fears seduction. Only one means of escape remains—death! Her father hands her the dagger only to snatch it from her again. Then she reminds him of that old Roman who killed his daughter to save her from disgrace. Odoardo obeys her command and stabs her. The prince passes judgment on the father, and banishes the wicked Marinelli with the words: "Go, hide thyself forever!"

Lessing's position as librarian at Wolfenbüttel was unsatisfactory; his salary was small and he desired to marry Eva König, the widow of a Hamburg friend. In 1775 he went to Vienna, where he had hoped to find a better position, but instead was compelled to accompany the Prince of Brunswick to Italy. After a year's absence, he returned to Wolfenbüttel, his salary was increased, and he married Eva; but his domestic joy was of short duration, for in a little more than a year his wife died and his heart was broken. During this time Lessing was engaged in serious theological controversies, in which he manifested remarkable ability in his discussions of religious questions, and aroused the whole theological world, especially Pastor Goeze of Hamburg, by the publication of the *Wolfenbütteler Fragmente* written by H. S. Reimarus, but published anonymously. The most important product of these controversies was the dramatic poem *Nathan der Weise*, which appeared in the year 1779.

NATHAN DER WEISE

This play, in which Lessing advocates religious tolerance, was first acted in Berlin in 1783, where it met with but little success; but when it was presented in Weimar in 1801, under the auspices of Goethe and Schiller, it was well received. A story found in the *Decamerone* of Boccaccio was the source of this drama, the scene being laid in Jerusalem at the time of the third crusade. The main interest of the drama centers in the parable of the three rings which represent the three religions, Mohammedanism, Judaism, and Christianity.

Act I. This act presents two sharply contrasted characters, Nathan the Jew, and the Patriarch of Jerusalem. Nathan, who has just returned from a business trip, learns that his beloved foster daughter, Recha, would have been burned to death during his absence had not a young Knight Templar rescued her, but that she is under the delusion that she was saved by an angel. A Dervish now comes to ask a loan for the Sultan, Saladin, who is in need of money. Nathan is very sympathetic, unprejudiced, and interested in all he hears. The Patriarch makes a far different impression upon us. He has sent a Friar to implicate the Templar in some villainy, although he knows that the Templar alone, out of twenty of his order, has been pardoned by the Sultan, because he reminds him of his brother. The Patriarch wishes him not only to spy out the weak places in the fortifications of Jerusalem and make them known to the crusaders, but to lie in wait for the Sultan, his benefactor, and kill him. The Patriarch, however, deceives himself in the Templar, for he is not adapted to play the part of a spy, nor does he share the view that "Villainy in the sight of man is not always villainy in the sight of God."

Act II. In this act the virtue of the Templar becomes more apparent. When he meets Nathan he declines all thanks for Recha's deliverance, and moreover does not hesitate to show his contempt for the Jew; yet he can not but appreciate the character of this honorable man. "Despise my race," says Nathan, "as much as you wish; neither of us has had any choice; are we our

race? What is a race? Are not Christians and Jews men?"
Humiliated, the Templar grasps Nathan's hand, and requests his
friendship. However, before Nathan can take him to his own
home he is summoned to appear before Saladin.

ACT III. The Sultan needs money, which he hopes to secure
through a scheme proposed by his sister, Sittah, but is disappointed. When, in order to entrap him, he asks Nathan which
of the three revealed religions is the true one, Nathan tells him
the parable of the rings. The story closes with the admonition of
the judge to the three brothers: "Well then, let each of you vie
with one another for uncorrupted love, free from prejudices. Let
each strive to reveal the power of the stone in his ring by gentle-
ness, kind forbearance, charity, and with hearty submission to
God!" Saladin is greatly touched by what he has heard, and in
an enthusiastic manner manifests his admiration for Nathan, who
has one request to make. He says that he has so much cash on
hand that he wishes the Sultan would make use of it. Like the
Templar, Saladin is humiliated by the Jew. Yet the time is close
at hand when both are to be perplexed by him. The Templar
has seen Recha and wishes to marry her, but Nathan hesitates to
give his consent. The Knight is astonished at this, and a deep
distrust is awakened in him when he learns through Daja that
Recha is the child of Christian parents, whom Nathan has reared
according to his faith.

ACT IV. The Templar consults the Patriarch without thinking
of the consequences, but is aroused when to all his remonstrances
the Patriarch says: "The Jew must be burned." In an interview
with Saladin, the passionate nature of the Templar is again made
manifest. He reproaches the man whose friendship he sought only
a short time before for having taken a Christian child for the purpose of rearing it in the Jewish faith, and the Sultan finally believes that the young man has good grounds for his suspicions.

The Friar soon explains Nathan's conduct in this affair. Nathan had, eighteen years before, lost his wife and seven sons
through the fury of the Christians. At that time a prominent
knight, Wolf von Filneck, sent him by his servant, the Friar, his
little daughter, because her mother had just died, and he himself
was obliged to go to war. Nathan, considering it a compensation

sent from heaven for his great loss, very gladly adopted the child, and reared her as his own. The thought, therefore, that he must now give up the child forever was most painful to him.

Act V. From a prayer book of the deceased Wolf von Filneck, which the Friar has carefully preserved, it is discovered that Recha and the Templar are brother and sister. Their father was Saladin's brother who, under the name of Filneck, had lived with his wife for some time in Germany. When on account of the climate the parents again returned to the Orient, they left their son in Germany under the care of Curd von Staufen, who gave the boy this name, and prevailed upon him to become a Templar. Nathan has the pleasure of seeing the Templar and his sister united with their uncle.

Soon after the completion of this work Lessing's health failed, and he died while on a visit in Brunswick in 1781. It has been truly said that Lessing lived far in advance of his time; that he was an advocate of religious toleration and modern thought; that he paved the way for the national drama and liberated the country from intellectual tyranny; that he manifested all those qualities which are characteristic of a noble, unselfish, and charitable nature.

THE PERIOD OF THE REVOLUTION

GERMAN literature was still under the influence of Voltaire, the patriotic efforts of Klopstock and the aesthetic principles of Lessing having not yet found general favor, when new influences came from France which produced in Germany an unexpected literary upheaval and revolution.

The reform in political, educational, and social conditions in France, brought on by the advocacy of Rousseau's ideas, was also destined to manifest itself in Germany. The reforms which seemed impracticable in the eighteenth century became the ideals of the poets in the next century and followed the movement called "Sturm und Drang." This agitation or manifestation of youthful vigor was at its highest in 1770–80 and advocated "originality and genius" in literature. Its representatives were intolerant of all rules and restrictions, and took the Volkslied, the Old Testament, Homer, Ossian, and Shakespeare as their models. JOHANN GEORG HAMANN, a theoretic writer on the true nature of poetry, became the center of the movement, and so interested Herder in his teachings that the latter became one of his stanchest adherents. Goethe, who was only twenty-one and had come under the influence of

Herder, was also imbued with the new spirit. His *Götz von Berlichingen*, which appeared soon afterward, was received as the first product of the new poetry in which the spirit of Shakespeare seemed to appear again. Goethe found imitators in the poets REINHOLD LENZ, MAXIMILIAN VON KLINGER, FRIEDRICH MÜLLER, and HEINRICH WAGNER. The new ideas were also applied to religion by JOHANN LAVATER, J. H. JUNG-STILLING, and FRIEDRICH H. JACOBI, and, in Württemberg, CHRISTIAN F. SCHUBART appeared as a representative of this movement against political servitude. Through Schubart's influence Schiller wrote his first dramas with which the "fermentation period" may be said to have reached its close for the present.

Among the great thinkers of the time we must mention IMMANUEL KANT, who through his doctrines of morality exerted a great influence on the intellectual life of this period; also JOHANN G. FICHTE, FRIEDRICH W. SCHELLING, and GEORG W. HEGEL,—each worked out his own theory of ethics, each thought his system of philosophy the true solution of all metaphysical problems.

In 1772, the "Göttinger Hain" was founded by a group of sentimental, excitable, and poetically inclined students who took Klopstock as their model. They disliked Wieland and agreed to "spread religion, virtue, emotion, and pure innocent wit." The *Göttinger Musenalmanach*, which had already

been published for three years, became the organ of
these poets and their friends, among whom were
HEINRICH C. BOIE, publisher of this journal, JO-
HANN H. VOSS, the STOLBERG brothers, LUDWIG H.
HÖLTY, J. MARTIN MILLER, MATTHIAS CLAUDIUS,
ANTON LEISEWITZ, FRIEDRICH W. GOTTER, and
GOTTFRIED A. BÜRGER.

Most of the poets of the "Hainbund," except Voss
and Bürger, were of mediocre ability and produced
nothing worthy of note. The former is remembered
by his idyls and his translations of Homer; the
latter, by his sonnets and ballads. Bürger's ballad
Lenore shows evidence of English influence and was
a stimulus to the Romantic movement in Europe.

JOHANN GOTTFRIED VON HERDER (1744–1803)

Johann G. von Herder was born in the village of
Mohrungen, East Prussia, August 25, 1744. His
youth was a series of troubles and privations. When
eighteen he entered the University of Königsberg,
and there he came under the influence of Kant and
Hamann, who prepared him for a position as teacher
in the "Domschule" at Riga. In the year 1769 he
decided to travel, as tutor, with the young Prince of
Holstein, and while at Darmstadt became acquainted
with Carolina Flachsland, whom he afterwards married. Weary of travel Herder remained at Strassburg during the winter of 1770–71 to undergo a
surgical operation on his eyes. Here he first met

Goethe, upon whom his influence was inestimable. He called Goethe's attention to Shakespeare and revealed to him the beauties of national poetry in the *Volkslieder*. An intimate friendship developed between the two men, and when in 1776 Herder longed for a wider field of activity, Goethe recommended him for the position of court chaplain and general superintendent of the church in Weimar. Here he published those works which have given him such a high rank in German literature. With the exception of a trip to Italy, Herder lived continuously in Weimar until his death in 1803.

Herder's reputation rests upon his scholarly ability as a translator, and as the author of many theological and philosophical writings, through which he became the most powerful advocate of religion, love, and friendship in Germany. His collection of *Volkslieder* taught the German people the full significance of their own past and stimulated a greater love for their own country.

His most widely known work is *Der Cid*, in which he Germanized Spanish romances and manifested his finest poetic achievement. Herder's most important book, *Ideen zur Philosophie der Geschichte der Menschheit*, in four parts, gives his conception of the evolution of mankind and shows how he endeavored to discover the laws which underlie it. This work, on which he spent seven years, gives evidence of his scientific knowledge and breadth of learning. Herder also published six volumes containing theological and educational treatises, didactic poems, legends, and mythological fables.

Johann Christoph Friedrich von Schiller
(1759–1805)

Johann Christoph Friedrich von Schiller was born at Marbach, Württemberg, November 10, 1759. His ancestors were of the middle class and were bakers and innkeepers. His father, Johann Kaspar, was a regimental surgeon, who finally rose to the rank of major. Schiller was four years old when the family moved to Lorch, and seven when they settled in Ludwigsburg. Here he attended the Latin School to prepare himself for his favorite study, theology. Karl Eugen, Duke of Württemberg, who was seeking promising students for his new military academy,—the later Karlsschule,—instituted in the palace "Solitude" near Ludwigsburg, offered Schiller a free education on condition that he serve the ducal House of Württemberg.

Schiller was therefore obliged to become a "Karlsschüler" when he was but fourteen years of age and to study jurisprudence, because theology was not taught there. Life at the academy was hateful to him. He could not endure the duke's tyrannical treatment, nor did he enjoy the strict military discipline and regulations of the school. His condition was somewhat improved when the school was transferred to Stuttgart, in November, 1775, and he took up the study of medicine. All the experiences at the academy served to kindle in the heart of this liberty-loving youth a hatred of tyranny, and to develop that spirit of independence which is so characteristic of the man. Schiller inclined more and more to the study of literature, especially poetry, and says of this time, "To escape from arrangements that tortured me, my heart sought refuge in the world of ideas, when as yet I was not acquainted with the world of realities, from which iron bars excluded me." Clandestinely he read the works of Rousseau, Ossian, Klopstock's *Messias*, Goethe's *Götz*, *Werther*, and *Clavigo;* also Wieland's translation of Shakespeare, which so awakened his own poetic impulse that he tried his hand at the drama, and three tragedies resulted: *Der Student von Nassau*, *Cosmus von Medici*, and *Die Räuber*, of which only the latter survives. Schiller left the academy December 15, 1780, entitled to practice as a physician.

Die Räuber

This drama, based upon a story by C. F. Schubart, was begun in the year 1777, published anonymously in 1781, and produced for the first time at Mannheim in 1782. It is a revolutionary tragedy and created a furore.

Act I. The two principal characters of the drama are two brothers, Karl, the prodigal son, and Franz, the hypocritical villain, who wishes to rob his brother of his inheritance and win the love of Amalie, his betrothed. Franz is the younger of the two sons of the old and weak Count Maximilian von Moor; he is ugly and repulsive in manner and loved by none; while Karl, on the other hand, is attractive in appearance, ambitious, and tender-hearted, although idle and quite frivolous. This disparity displeases Franz, and he devises a plan to carry out his evil purpose. He reads to his father a letter ostensibly coming from a friend of the family, but written by himself, in which he describes Karl as a wicked, indifferent student at the University of Leipzig, who, with seven other students, has been compelled to leave the city to escape the law. Franz so influences his father that he is authorized to write to his brother that his father does not wish to see him again until he has reformed. The villain now thinks his plan has succeeded, but he is disappointed in Amalie, who sees through the scheme and remains true to her lover. We next find Karl on the boundary of Saxony. He has fled from Leipzig, and has penitently written his father for pardon, but the answer comes from his brother that he must never show himself again in his home or he will be thrown into the tower. When Karl reads this letter he is filled with despair, and renounces all faith in humanity. One of his companions proposes to organize a band of robbers with Karl as leader. Believing that they can in this way restore justice in the world, they withdraw to the Bohemian forests.

Act II. This act describes the life of this robber band, and also shows how far Franz has progressed in wickedness. To hasten the death of his father he has the news carried through his accomplice Hermann that Karl has been killed in the battle of Prague. This so overcomes the father that he becomes unconscious and is believed to be dead. The robbers are described as men fearless of death, who love liberty more than honor and life, but hate tyranny. They are everywhere welcomed by the poor and the oppressed. Karl is exceedingly kind to widows and orphans, with whom he shares his booty, but he is a veritable demon when he comes in contact with a rich man or an oppressor of the people. In attempting to surround the robbers the soldiers are overcome; only Roller, Karl's most faithful friend, is slain.

Act III. The death of Roller deeply affects Karl, and when he learns how bravely the robbers have fought for him, he declares that he will never forsake them. But soon thoughts of home and Amalie come over him with increased power, and with his band he sets out for Franconia. Amalie has learned from Hermann, who regrets the part which he has played in this wicked scheme, that her lover and the old count still live.

ACT IV. Under an assumed name Karl now comes to the castle of his brother. His father's old servant recognizes him immediately, and Franz also surmises who the visitor is. His conscience troubles him and he resolves to poison his guest. But Amalie, who feels herself irresistibly drawn to the newcomer, does not recognize her lover. In the night Karl returns to the robbers, who have encamped near an old ruined castle. Tormented by thoughts of suicide and not able to rest, he hears a voice down in the dark dungeon. He breaks open the door and drags out his poor father, who for three months has been languishing in this prison. Apparently dead, he had been placed in a coffin, and when he regained consciousness Franz had him thrown into the tower to die; but the sympathetic Hermann had at the risk of his own life saved him. When Karl hears this he is greatly enraged at his brother and threatens to take revenge. He commands that the murderer be captured alive and brought before him.

ACT V. We next find Franz struggling with his own conscience; the description of his dream of the judgment, the interview with Pastor Moser concerning the immortality of the soul, his vain attempt to pray, and the suicide of the villain, give evidence of Schiller's great dramatic genius.

The close of the play shows how justice asserts itself even in the life of a robber. The robbers bring the body of Franz, and also Amalie, who has meanwhile been informed of what has taken place in the forest, to their leader. When the father learns the identity of his rescuer he dies, and Amalie is at her own wish killed by her lover, who, according to his oath, can not leave the robbers.

Finally the awful consequences of his deeds appear to Karl and he cries out in despair: "O fool that I was to think that I could better the world by deeds of violence, and enforce the laws by lawlessness! . . . . Here I now stand at the close of a terrible life and have to realize with wailing and gnashing of teeth that two such

men as I can overthrow the whole structure of the moral world."
A prize of one thousand louis d'ors is offered for his capture,
and to allow a poor man to secure it he surrenders himself to
him.

After leaving the Karlsschule Schiller was appointed regimental surgeon at Stuttgart by the duke;
but his salary was small and he was still under the
strictest discipline. The publication of *Die Räuber*
was an expensive burden and, at the time, dangerous
on account of its revolutionary tone, for Schiller still
remembered the fate of his friend Schubart, who for a
similar offense was imprisoned in the castle of Hohen-
asperg for ten years. On January 13, 1782, Schiller
stole away to Mannheim to see his first drama played,
and was gratified with its reception. The duke now
commanded Schiller to cease "all literary work and
all communication with other countries," and when
Schiller for the second time went to Mannheim, he
had him put under arrest for fourteen days.

Encouraged by the hopes held out to him by Dalberg, the manager of the Mannheim Court Theater,
Schiller resolved upon flight. Accompanied by his
friend, Andreas Streicher, he left Stuttgart in the
night of September 22, 1782, under the assumed name
of Dr. Schmidt and went directly to Mannheim.
Here he was doomed to disappointment and financial
embarrassment. Dalberg was not ready to assist
him, and, besides, Schiller felt insecure. Streicher,
however, was willing to share his funds with him and

they took refuge at Oggersheim, near Mannheim,
until Schiller had revised and completed his next
drama, *Fiesco*. Fearing that even here he was not
safe from the duke's anger, he accepted the invitation of Frau von Wolzogen, the mother of one of
his fellow students, to make his home with her in
Bauerbach. Here, during the winter of 1782, he
completed *Kabale und Liebe* and planned *Don Carlos*.
Dalberg, attracted by this drama, invited Schiller to
return to Mannheim as "Theater Poet," but the
small salary and continued illness caused him to resign at the end of the first year. He next turned
to journalism and founded *Die Rheinische Thalia*,
which gave him greater literary influence, but was
financially a failure.

At this time Duke Karl August, of Weimar, to
whom Schiller had read parts of *Don Carlos*, conferred upon him the title of Hofrat (court counselor)
but this did not relieve him of financial straits. This
relief was left to his ardent admirer, Christian Gottfried Körner, father of the poet, Karl Theodor Körner, who invited Schiller to come to Leipzig, where a
new life was to open for him.

Fiesco

This play, which was written in prose, was performed in Mannheim, January, 1784, under the title
*Die Verschwörung des Fiesco zu Genua, ein Repub-
likanisches Trauerspiel*. As a political drama, it

is a glorification of Republican ideas; but since there was no inclination toward political freedom in Germany at the time, the play was not as well received as *Die Räuber*. Although a tragedy of a state as well as of an individual, its characters are superior to those in the preceding drama. The scene is laid in Genoa in the year 1547.

ACT I. The Doge of Genoa, the honorable and affable Andreas Doria, has displeased his people by allowing his dissolute nephew, Gianettino, his probable successor, too much authority and influence. Verrina, an old, stubborn republican, plans a conspiracy, but only Fiesco, the Count of Lavagna, is capable of being the leader. He, however, does not appear to concern himself with the affairs of his country, apparently considering feasts of more importance. He even goes so far as to carry on a love affair with Julia, the disreputable sister of Gianettino, thus seeking to conceal his ambitious designs. Fiesco hopes in this way to make his cause more secure and to put himself at the head of the state. Gianettino fears Fiesco, who, like a magnet, attracts the dissatisfied element to himself. He sends the sly and bold Moor Hassan to kill Fiesco, who, however, is on the watch, disarms his would-be assassin, and secures him for his own service.

ACT II. The time has now come for Fiesco to act. The dissatisfaction which Gianettino's overbearing conduct at the election of a procurator and judges of the peace has caused gives Fiesco an excuse for arousing the nobility and people to a general uprising and revolution. He allows the Moor to wound him and then drags him before the court to confess that he has been bribed by the prince. When the people have been thus aroused against the house of Doria, Fiesco begs to have the Moor pardoned. When Gianettino hears of this, he prepares to have the German troops enter the city within two days; Fiesco and twelve senators are to be put to death, and Gianettino himself is to rule in place of his uncle. Fiesco has also prepared himself for an emergency, having summoned four galleys and two thousand men to serve him;

but he is still undecided whether he ought to free Genoa or place himself at the head of the state.

ACT III. After a restless night Fiesco decides to seek the ducal crown, and fortune seems to favor him. The Moor has come into the possession of a document which reveals Gianettino's plans, and he also confesses that he has been commissioned by Julia to poison Fiesco's wife, the faithful and virtuous Leonore. The conspirators have now sufficient cause for proceeding, but Verrina has seen through Fiesco's scheme and resolves that he must die.

ACT IV. Preparations are now completed for the insurrection; the leaders and soldiers are already assembled at Fiesco's court, when the news comes that the Moor whom Fiesco had dismissed, since he thought he had no further use for him, has betrayed the conspiracy to the Doge. This rumor is confirmed when the Doge, soon thereafter, magnanimously sends the Moor in bonds to Fiesco, who immediately releases him. A final attempt is made by Leonore to persuade her husband to desist from his plans, but in vain, for at this moment a shot gives the signal for the uprising.

ACT V. Fiesco, who does not wish to be outdone in generosity by the Doge, now hastens to warn him. The Doge flees when his German bodyguard corroborates the news of the insurrection, but soon returns, believing that the Genoese will not desert him thus and drive him into a foreign land in his eightieth year. Meanwhile the Moor has been seized and hanged as an incendiary, and Gianettino has been slain by one of the conspirators. When Leonore, who in her anxiety for her husband wanders through the streets in male attire, comes upon the corpse of Gianettino, she takes off his scarlet robe and hangs it about her shoulders; and so it happens that conflicting reports are circulated concerning the death of the prince, and Leonore is stabbed by her own husband. Stirred to greater deeds by the death of his wife, Fiesco hastens to the Signoria to be proclaimed Duke. Clothed in purple robes, he meets Verrina on the way to the harbor. When the usurper will not listen to Verrina's friendly advice the old patriot decides that Fiesco must die at once. As ruler, Fiesco first of all resolves to free the galley slaves, but just as he is about to cross the bridge to the ship, Verrina thrusts him into the sea. At the same time one of the conspirators hurries to Verrina with the news that Andreas

Doria has returned and that Genoa is giving him a glad welcome. Verrina also goes to greet and serve his old master again.

KABALE UND LIEBE

This bourgeois tragedy was first presented on the stage in April, 1784. The original title of the play was *Luise Millerin*, but it was changed at the suggestion of the poet and actor Iffland, of Mannheim. It is written in prose and has as its leading thought class prejudice and corruption at the princely courts.

ACT I. Luise, the daughter of the town musician Miller, loves Ferdinand, the son of President von Walter, who has by unjust methods become minister of a petty German court. The attention which the young major is paying Luise, encouraged by her short-sighted mother, does not please her father, who thinks more of honor than of personal gain. Luise, a type of the virtuous maiden of the middle class, clings with the passion of youth to Ferdinand, who, in spite of the wickedness of the court, has kept himself pure, and hopes to overcome all the difficulties and marry Luise. The proud president and his secretary, Wurm, skilled in intrigue and incapable of believing in true love, have a united interest in preventing the marriage. The president wishes his son to marry Lady Milford, a rejected mistress of the prince, so that the president's influence may be strengthened at the court; and Wurm desires to marry Luise. Accustomed to act quickly, the president sends von Kalb, a low-minded simpleton, to make known at the "Residenz" that Lady Milford is to marry his son, and at the same time he commands Ferdinand to seek her hand without delay. Ferdinand is determined to thwart his father's plans, and hopes to induce Lady Milford to reject him.

ACT II. Lady Milford appears to be a far different person than Ferdinand thought. Although she has been ambitious to be the first lady of the court, she has used her influence to relieve poor subjects. Ferdinand had intended to reproach her for wrongdoing, but when she confesses her love for him, his attitude toward her is changed. The danger which threatens Luise and Ferdinand seems now to have increased. The president comes with officers to Miller's home to arrest Luise and put her in the pillory, but Ferdinand, who happens to be present, resists them. When he sees that he can not turn his father from his purpose he threatens to disclose secrets which will be detrimental to the president; this has the desired effect.

Act III. We now find the president exceedingly angry because his plans have miscarried, and his secretary evolves a diabolical plan. Finding that force will not avail, suspicion is used to transform love into destructive jealousy. Luise is separated from her parents; her father is thrown into the tower, ostensibly because he has insulted the president, and her mother is taken to a spinning house. They are to receive their freedom only on condition that Luise writes a letter, at Wurm's dictation, in which she appears to be carrying on an intrigue with von Kalb. This letter falls into Ferdinand's hands, and he at once plans revenge on von Kalb.

Act IV. Ferdinand sends for von Kalb and challenges him to a duel, but he is too cowardly, and confesses that he does not even know Luise. Ferdinand's wrath now turns against the unfortunate girl. She meanwhile has had an interview with Lady Milford, who sees in the musician's daughter a harmless creature unworthy to be considered her rival. But Lady Milford has soon to learn that her own charming appearance is not comparable with innocence of heart and with that maturity of character which is produced by misfortune. The burgher maiden shows her superiority over the woman of noble birth and consents to renounce her lover. Lady Milford, however, does not wish to be outdone,—she, too, has a great soul. To save the loving couple she resolves to leave the principality forever; but her magnanimity is shown too late.

Act V. At the bidding of her father, Luise has given up her intention of committing suicide, and wishes now to flee with him to another country, but before this can be done Ferdinand appears. The thought that Luise has betrayed him has overpowered every other feeling, and he has come for the purpose of poisoning both himself and Luise. He demands that she confess whether she has written the letter, and when, in accordance with her oath, she is obliged to admit it, he asks for a glass of lemonade, into which he puts the poison. While Luise is preparing the drink, Ferdinand sends her father to the president's home with a letter in which he tells what he has done. The last moments of the lovers are very touching, for when Luise finds that she must die she confesses her innocence, and discloses the name of the guilty one. She has scarcely breathed her last when the president, von Wurm, and a great crowd enter and learn the truth. As Ferdinand dies he cries out to his father: "I have been treacherously robbed of my life through you!" The conscience of the president is now aroused, for he feels the guilt of having loaded a dual murder upon his son. He curses his evil adviser, and attempts to wash his own hands of guilt; but the sight of the two corpses so affects von Wurm that he resolves to surrender himself to the arm of justice. Ferdinand extends his hand to his father in token of forgiveness.

DON CARLOS

According to the first sketch which Schiller made of this play at Bauerbach in 1783, it was to represent a domestic tragedy in a princely family. During the four years that intervened a new idea was introduced in the character of Marquis Posa, who, as a second hero, represents freedom of thought and the dignity of man in contradistinction to monarchical and ecclesiastical despotism. This drama, written in iambic blank verse in 1787, is also revolutionary in character.

ACT I. Don Carlos is a visionary, frank, and thoughtless young man, just the opposite of his father, Philip II., of Spain, who is a suspicious despot, feared by his subjects and estranged from his own family. Carlos' stepmother, the beautiful and intellectual Elizabeth of Valois, had been betrothed to him before his father took her for his own bride. As time passes, Carlos' love for her increases to such a degree that the father becomes suspicious. Marquis Posa, a true friend of Carlos, has opportunely returned

from the Netherlands to the Spanish court. He cares nothing
for princely favor and power; his heart longs for the welfare of
humanity. He has seen the wretchedness of the enslaved provinces
of Flanders and seeks to gain the good will of Carlos to assist him
in their deliverance. The service which Posa asks of Carlos seems
to be the best means of curing him of his love for Elizabeth, who,
though not insensible to the love of the prince, acquiesces in Posa's
plan.

Act II. Elizabeth's indorsement suffices to encourage Carlos
to free Flanders, but in vain he requests the king to appoint him
governor of the Netherlands. Philip's selfish counselors,—his
confessor, the untrustworthy and underhanded Domingo, and the
proud and ambitious General Alba,—fill his heart with suspicion,
so that he fears to give his son the weapons for a rebellion. The
prince's enemies are not satisfied with the refusal of the appointment, but seek, if possible, his destruction, for Alba hates him and
Domingo fears in him a regent who *thinks*, and therefore might
destroy the power of the church. Chance seems to favor them; a
lady in waiting of the queen, the passionate and frivolous Princess
Eboli, loves Carlos and invites him to an interview. He thinks
that it is the queen who has invited him and confesses his disappointment, thereby betraying the secret of his love. This soon
reaches the ears of Domingo.

Act III. At the suggestion of Domingo, Eboli takes some letters
and a medallion of the prince from a strong box which belongs to
the queen, and gives them to the confessor. Philip believes himself deceived, and his advisers increase his suspicions to such an
extent that the king himself begins to doubt their sincerity, and
longs for some one in whom he can confide. He consults his
records, and his eyes fall upon a name that he has once under-
scored, for some reason now forgotten. Marquis Posa is the man
he needs as his counselor in this affair; but the marquis declines,
saying that he can not be the servant of a prince. He then sets
forth his ideas of man's dignity and worth, which in Schiller's time
found an echo in the hearts of thousands. The king is not offended, believing that he knows mankind better than does Posa.
The marquis finally complies with the king's earnest entreaties,
thinking he may in this position be better able to assist his young

friend, and also further his own purposes. The king gives him the authority to learn the relations between the queen and the prince.

ACT IV. Posa believes he can best serve the king by deceiving him. Carlos is to go secretly to Brussels and become the leader of a rebellion; his father will then voluntarily give him the position which he has requested, and Flanders will be saved. Posa makes his plan known to the queen, who is to disclose it to the prince; but it is thwarted by Carlos himself. The kind but too officious Count Lerma, who, as head of the king's bodyguard, is always near the king, has overheard the interview with Posa, and excites the prince's suspicion. Carlos believes he has been betrayed, and when Posa asks him for his pocketbook, which contains a letter which might expose the queen, the prince hastens to warn her. Posa appears just as Carlos is opening his heart to the Princess Eboli and begging her to secure for him an interview with the queen. The secret is now made public, and Carlos seems to be lost; but his friend still hopes to save him by sacrificing himself for him. He has the prince imprisoned, so that he will not take any thoughtless steps, and then writes a letter, addressed to William of Orange,—for he knows that all letters for Flanders are given over to the king,—in which he appears as the guilty person; he asserts that he himself has loved the queen and through the monarch has found a way to approach her freely; fearing that he might be betrayed by Carlos he has had him imprisoned, and he himself is now ready to flee to Brussels. The letter falls into the king's hands, and Posa's doom is sealed.

ACT V. During the last interview with Carlos a shot through the prison gate kills the marquis. Indescribable is the grief of Carlos, fearful the shock when the king learns the true state of affairs. Meanwhile the queen has devised a way of escape for the prince; he is to take the mail coach which will await him at a Carthusian monastery; but before he leaves he is to pass through the palace halls at midnight in the form of the dead emperor, and visit the queen in her apartments. But not only are all the preparations for flight disclosed, even the plans which Carlos was to carry out when he reached the Netherlands are discovered. The king is still in doubt whether he ought to allow his son to flee or not. The Grand Inquisitor answers the question for him, and Don Carlos

is captured in the queen's apartments and given over to the executioner.

Schiller went to Leipzig in the spring of 1785,
where he found in Körner a true friend, who not
only provided a home for him in Leipzig and Gohlis,
and later in Dresden and Loschwitz, but who also
relieved him of all financial cares and enabled him
to pursue his studies in philosophy and history.
During this time he wrote for the *Thalia*, finished
Don Carlos, and composed a number of excellent
lyrics, of which his ode *An die Freude* is the best.
His study of history led him to begin the *Geschichte
des Abfalls der Niederlande*, and he continued to
work on a romance, *Der Geisterseher*. A visit to
Weimar in 1787 brought him into touch with many
prominent people, and gave him an opportunity to
visit the University of Jena. In Rudolstadt he became acquainted with Charlotte von Lengefeld, and
here about a year later he met Goethe, who helped
him to obtain a professorship of history in the University of Jena, where he gave his first lecture in
May, 1789. The following February he married
Charlotte at the little church at Wenigenjena. Although Schiller and Goethe had met in 1788, they did
not become intimate friends until 1794. Schiller's
ability as a historian manifested itself in the *Geschichte des dreissigjährigen Krieges*, and in his historical dramas which followed. But again his activity
was checked by illness and financial embarrassment;

this time help came from an unexpected source; the Duke of Holstein, Friedrich von Augustenburg, and Count von Schimmelmann learned of his destitution, and generously offered him a thousand thalers a year for three years, so that he was able to make a trip to Karlsbad and to visit his old home in Württemberg. After he had finished his *Geschichte des dreissigjährigen Krieges*, he gave himself up more completely to the study of Kant's philosophy. Schiller's most important work on aesthetics, the *Briefe über die ästhetische Erziehung des Menschen*, was published in his new journal, *Die Horen*, in which Goethe took a very active interest. Owing perhaps to the poor taste of the public, *Die Horen* did not prove a success and Goethe and Schiller were criticised, but they retaliated by writing a collection of satiric epigrams, called *Xenien*, which were published in Schiller's *Musenalmanach* for 1796. Criticism was, for a time at least, silenced; the air was cleared, and both poets felt it incumbent on them to follow up their victory with some great and worthy work of art.

In the following year, which is called the ballad year, appeared the following ballads: *Der Taucher, Der Handschuh, Der Ring des Polykrates, Ritter Toggenburg, Die Kraniche des Ibykus*, and *Der Gang nach dem Eisenhammer*. These were followed at intervals by *Der Kampf mit dem Drachen, Die Bürgschaft, Hero und Leander*, and *Der Graf von Habs-*

burg. All these ballads express noble sentiment and illustrate some principle of moral conduct.

As a poet Schiller evinced great ability. His poems reveal not only the purity and beauty of his own character, but also the purest poetic ideals combined with true artistic form and language. He was an idealist of the highest type. His fondness for the lyric and his ability to give expression to tender feelings and emotions are seen to good advantage in the *Reiterlied* in *Wallenstein's Lager*, the *Fischer-*, *Hirten-* and *Jägerlied* in *Wilhelm Tell*, *Des Mädchens Klage*, *Der Jüngling am Bache*, and many other poems. Reflective and noble are the sentiments expressed in the so-called "Ideendichtung," which may be divided into four classes:

1. Symbolical narratives or poems which present human experiences in narrative form, as *Pegasus im Joche*, *Die Teilung der Erde*, *Das verschleierte Bild zu Sais*, *Kassandra*, *Das Siegesfest*, and *Der Alpenjäger*.

2. Symbolical descriptions. These poems show the development of an idea in the description of some real or imaginary event, as *Der Spaziergang*, *Das Eleusische Fest*, *Die Macht des Gesanges*, and *Das Lied von der Glocke*, the most famous of all his poems. It is a vivid and charming picture of life from the cradle to the grave, together with a description of the making of the bell; it was written in 1799.

3. Allegories, in which some thought or idea is

represented by poetic word painting, as *Das Mädchen aus der Fremde* and *Der Pilgrim*.

4. Aphorisms, which express certain ideas in a simple and unstilted form, as *Hoffnung, Die Worte des Glaubens, Die Worte des Wahns,* and *Sprüche des Confucius*.

From this time on Schiller continued his labors indefatigably, and produced in rapid succession *Wallenstein* (1798–99), *Maria Stuart* (1801), *Die Jungfrau von Orleans* (1802), *Die Braut von Messina* (1803), and *Wilhelm Tell* (1804). Schiller provided the German stage also with the translations of *Macbeth, Turandot, Der Parasit, Der Neffe als Onkel,* and *Phädra*. This restless activity was sure to find its reward, for everywhere his writings were eagerly sought and read. In 1799 Schiller took up his residence in Weimar, where he could devote more time to his literary labors and enjoy an increased income from the Grand Duke Karl August, who also secured from the emperor Schiller's elevation to the rank of nobility,—an honor which was greatly appreciated by the family. Efforts were made to attract Schiller to Berlin, where he and his family visited in the spring of 1804, but Weimar offered inducements which he could not well resist. His frail constitution could not stand the tremendous strain and his health gradually failed. Schiller's last tragedy, *Demetrius*, and other work which he had planned were left unfinished. On the 29th of April he was taken seriously ill in the theater, and he died on the evening of May 9, 1805, at the age of forty-five, mourned by the whole nation. In 1827 his body was exhumed and placed in the ducal vault where it rests at the side of Goethe and Karl August.

WALLENSTEIN

Schiller had for years cherished the idea of representing the life of Wallenstein in dramatic form. Finally on account of the extensive plot which he wished to present, he decided to divide it into three parts: *Wallensteins Lager*, as an introductory play, and two five-act dramas, *Die Piccolomini* and *Wallensteins Tod;* the former gives the exposition in all its fullness, while the latter is in itself a complete tragedy. *Wallensteins Lager* was put upon the Weimar stage in October, 1798; *Die Piccolomini*, in January, 1799, and *Wallensteins Tod*, in the following April.

This trilogy may be regarded as the greatest and most complete tragedy in the literature of the eighteenth century.

WALLENSTEINS LAGER

In this prologue we obtain a panoramic view of the soldiers of the Thirty Years' War. In the camp before Pilsen we see the ruined peasant who seeks to repair his fortune by gambling with loaded dice; the self-conscious sergeant, who thinks he knows more than other people; the simple Croat, who allows the sharp-shooter to get the better of him; Gustel von Blasewitz, the buxom sutler woman; the spirited Capuchin Friar, and the noble-minded Cuirassier, whose stirring song: "Wohlauf Kameraden, aufs

Pferd, aufs Pferd!" is still a national favorite. This heterogeneous army, which is held together only by the powerful name of Wallenstein, forms the background of the two dramas.

Die Piccolomini

Act I. Von Questenberg, the imperial envoy, has come to Wallenstein's camp to ask him to evacuate Bohemia, and to send a detachment of eight regiments of horse to the Spanish Prince Cardinal. He is at the same time to ascertain the fidelity of Wallenstein's officers and soldiers, for it has been rumored in Vienna that the great commander is not loyal to his sovereign. The insolent manner in which Questenberg is received by the generals does not tend to reassure him. Lieutenant General Octavio Piccolomini, a resolute, double-faced man, does not hesitate to cast suspicion upon his commander, and makes use of the implicit confidence which Wallenstein places in him to find out his plans, that he may betray them to the emperor. But Max, his son, is a youthful idealist, who clings to his leader with absolute devotion, and even Questenberg can not destroy his faith in him.

Act II. We now find Wallenstein, Duke of Friedland, at the height of his power. His one aim, in which he is abetted by his sister-in-law, Countess Terzky, is his own aggrandizement. He is a firm believer in astrology, for the stars have foretold his greatness. His clear, penetrating mind, cold reserve, and commanding presence have gained the respect and devotion of the great army which he has himself created, and upon which he relies for help in securing the goal of his ambition, the crown of Bohemia. To this end, however, it is necessary for him to enter into an alliance with the Swedes; but he is unwilling to do this without first consulting the stars. Up to this time all negotiations have been carried on by the unscrupulous Field Marshal Illo and Wallenstein's brother-in-law, Count Terzky. They now urge the duke to act, but he only answers, "The time has not yet come." In his conversation with Questenberg, Wallenstein plays the part of the injured one, and declares in the presence of his generals that he is willing to resign his leadership, for he knows that this threat, more than anything else, will bind the officers more closely to him.

Act III. This act presents the idealism of love in contrast with the intrigues of selfish ambition. The lovers, Thekla, Wallenstein's daughter, and Max Piccolomini, are not historical characters. Thekla, like Max, despises intrigue, but she is a shrewder observer than he, and discovers in her aunt, the Countess Terzky, a schemer who favors the love-affair only to unite Max's fate with Wallenstein's. She is suspicious of her own father, and warns her lover not to confide too much in men.

Act IV. Illo has undertaken to obtain the signatures of the generals, pledging them to follow their commander, even though he prove a traitor to the emperor; but this can only be done under false pretenses. At a banquet given by Terzky, a document is presented to the officers in which they declare their loyalty to the duke, "in so far as the oath to the emperor will permit." After all have read this it is exchanged for a copy omitting the important clause, and it is then unhesitatingly signed by the half-intoxicated officers. Two men, however, are not blind to the deception,— Octavio Piccolomini, and Colonel Buttler, but they also sign the paper; the one to conceal his duplicity, the other out of hostility to the emperor, who, he fancies, has insulted him. Max alone does not sign his name, preferring to "defer the business until the next day."

Act V. Octavio informs Max of Wallenstein's treason and shows him a full imperial patent by which Octavio is empowered, at the first step which the duke shall openly take against his sovereign, to depose him and himself assume command of the army. These disclosures tend rather to lessen Max's confidence in his father than to destroy his ideal of his hero. Even the report that Sesina, Wallenstein's messenger to the Swedes, has been captured, does not convince the young enthusiast, and he hastens to learn the truth from the duke's own lips.

WALLENSTEINS TOD

Act I. The capture of Sesina forces the duke to decide whether he will submit to the emperor, or openly desert him. The network of fate is fast closing in around him, and all circumstances seem united to incriminate him. He casts his lot with the Swedes, for the stars, which he has been observing with old Seni, the astrologer, seem to favor this course.

ACT II. To Octavio Wallenstein blindly intrusts an important position, which this faithless friend naturally turns to his own advantage. Before he leaves the camp he wins over to himself most of the officers, but Buttler hesitates. Not until Octavio shows him a letter written by Wallenstein to the imperial minister, in which he opposes Buttler's advancement, does he consent to leave him. Buttler now becomes Wallenstein's mortal enemy, and longs for revenge. In the touching farewell scene between father and son, Max refuses to accompany his father, but assures him, "Unworthy of thee wilt thou never see me."

ACT III. Nemesis follows fast on Wallenstein's footsteps. Regiment after regiment leaves him and swears allegiance anew to the emperor. But the hardest blow comes when Max, after a fierce inward struggle, forsakes him and proves his loyalty to his emperor by leading a wild charge against the Swedes, in which he seeks and finds a soldier's death. Only Buttler, whom the duke has been somewhat inclined to distrust, pretends to remain true to him. But the first news which his false friend brings him is that Prague is lost; that the Bohemian cities have gone over to the emperor, and that Wallenstein himself is accused of treachery.

ACT IV. Fortune seems again to smile upon the duke, who has escaped to the fortress in Eger. The Swedes have successfully repulsed the attack of Max Piccolomini, and will within twenty-four hours join the duke, who thus sees a new road to victory open to him; but already death and destruction hover over him. Buttler had expected to imprison the duke in Eger, but his plans are frustrated by the approach of the Swedes, and he resolves upon Wallenstein's death.

ACT V. Evil omens warn the hero of his death; Countess Terzky has evil dreams concerning him, and an ominous change is also noticed in the planets. When Seni urges him to break with the Swedes, Wallenstein says: "The warning should have come before! At present I need no revelation from the stars." Wallenstein has scarcely retired when Buttler, who has just returned from the murder of Terzky and Illo at a banquet, comes to dispatch Wallenstein also. The commander of the citadel begs him to wait, but in a few moments the deed is done. Almost at the same time Octavio enters with all his train to capture the duke. The "House of Splendor, and of princely glory, doth now stand desolated," for the duchess is dying, the countess takes poison, and Thekla flees to die at the grave of her lover.

Maria Stuart

Soon after the completion of *Wallenstein* Schiller began his preliminary work on *Maria Stuart*, and in June, 1800, it was presented in Weimar. The poet did not wish to represent the Scottish queen and her time according to history, but rather to present a woman whose fate it is to experience and enkindle strong passions. Although the plot is simple and compact, the play is too sentimental to be classed among his best dramas.

Act I. Mary Stuart, who, on account of a Scottish insurrection, has fled to England, is imprisoned in the castle at Fotheringay. The beautiful but unfortunate queen, repenting of her criminal past, on the anniversary of the murder of Darnley, her second husband, receives the news that she has been found guilty of instigating a conspiracy against the life of Queen Elizabeth. Conscious of her innocence, she is convinced that the English queen and her counselors wish her death, and that only the fear of being accused of cruelty hinders Elizabeth from carrying out the death sentence. Only one person, Count Leicester, Elizabeth's favorite, can save Mary. Mortimer, a hot-blooded, foolhardy youth, a nephew of the jailor, becomes her messenger to Leicester.

Act II. Elizabeth is serious and faithful in the discharge of her duties, but vain and revengeful, and can not decide to pardon Mary, as sympathetic old Talbot advises, nor is she willing to have her led to the scaffold, as the unfeeling Burleigh, who subordinates his conscience to the interests of the state, wishes. She believes that Mortimer is the man who can help her out of her predicament. The young man apparently acquiesces in her wishes, only to be the better able to prepare for Mary's deliverance. He discloses his plan to Leicester, to whom he brings a letter and a picture of Mary. But he is disappointed; for, instead of finding in Leicester a resolute man who would surmount all difficulties to save the unhappy queen, he finds him a cowardly and double-tongued courtier. Leicester loves Mary, but the hope of becoming Elizabeth's husband has caused him to feign love for the English queen, and to keep himself aloof from her rival. Now, when the engagement of Elizabeth to a French prince is imminent, his interest in Mary is more apparent. However, he does not wish to become a party to Mortimer's plan, preferring craftily to hinder Elizabeth from signing the death warrant. He thinks if he can bring about a meeting of the queens the execution can be prevented; "for the royal presence brings favor." He persuades Elizabeth, by flattering her vanity, to consent to meet Mary.

ACT III. The two hostile queens meet as it were accidentally in the garden of the castle at Fotheringay. Mary expects a friendly advance from her victorious enemy; Elizabeth, humble subjection from her sorely tried rival. The queenly manner of the prisoner only irritates the proud and overbearing English queen, who is not satisfied to see her enemy in the dust before her, but seems to delight in her misfortune and does not hesitate to abuse her in the most shameful manner. The old hatred is again awakened in Mary's breast and she has the satisfaction of knowing that she has deeply wounded the feelings of the queen. To hasten Mary's fate an attempt on Elizabeth's life is made while she is returning from London, which is, however, frustrated by Talbot.

ACT IV. Danger and destruction now seem to threaten Leicester. The queen receives from Lord Burleigh Mary's unfinished letter to Leicester, in which she promises him her hand in marriage. Leicester tries to save himself by a bold stroke. He has Mortimer, who has come to warn him, imprisoned, and informs Elizabeth that he had begun the correspondence with Mary merely to find out her plans. But he can not justify himself, since Mortimer, upon whom he relied for acquittal, has during his imprisonment committed suicide. Leicester, therefore, to save himself, is obliged to advise Mary's immediate execution, and it becomes his sad duty to see to it that the death sentence is carried out.

ACT V. After Mary has said farewell to her female attendants and confessed for the last time, Burleigh and Leicester come to prepare her for her end. At the sight of her betrayer Mary for a moment loses her self-control, but soon recovers and bids him farewell. Her confession that she had loved him and intended to marry him completely crushes the wretched man, whom still harder trials await. He has not the courage to witness Mary's execution. The sounds which reach his room make it almost unendurable for him to remain, and he attempts to flee. The door, however, is locked and he is forced to endure this gruesome proceeding until he loses consciousness. Elizabeth meanwhile is in doubt as to whether the execution has taken place, and her conscience troubles her so that all joy over the death of her rival is taken away. When Talbot informs her that one of the witnesses, who claimed that Mary was guilty, has confessed in a delirium that he had sworn falsely, Elizabeth wishes to have a new trial. It is, however, too late, for Burleigh brings the news that Mary is dead. To free herself from the appearance of crime she banishes the overzealous Burleigh. Talbot resigns his office and leaves her with the words: "I am too old, and this sincere hand is too stiff to put the seal on thy new deeds." Leicester takes voluntary flight to France, and the queen stands alone in her sorrowful plight.

DIE JUNGFRAU VON ORLEANS

This drama, described by Schiller as a "Romantic tragedy," takes us back to the time when France suffered the greatest humiliation (1429–30). The chief characters are types rather than individuals, and the play in many respects resembles an opera. It was completed in April, 1801, and is in every particular a finer work than *Maria Stuart*.

The prologue shows the distressed condition of France, and acquaints us with the early history of Jeanne d'Arc, the youngest daughter of a rich peasant of the village of Dom Remy. Her father wishes to see his daughters married before the English invaders reach their home, but Johanna rejects Raimond, her lover, although he is the best young man in the village, and absolutely devoted to her. She has prayed to the Virgin to save France from the English, and the Virgin has appeared to her bearing a sword and a banner. She is wholly engrossed in the affairs of her country, and her strange conduct causes her family much anxiety. When the news reaches them that the Duke of Burgundy and Isabeau, the king's own mother, have allied themselves with the English and that the entire force of the enemy is before Orleans, she believes it her divine mission to liberate her people, and leaves her home for the court of the Dauphin at Chinon.

Act I. Johanna now appears as a prophetess. When Charles VII, a kind but weak regent, who has been leading a pastoral life with the lovely Agnes Sorrel far from the scenes of war, learns of the misfortune which has befallen France, he wishes to prevent further bloodshed by yielding to the enemy. In vain does the hot-tempered Dunois seek to awaken his sense of honor; in vain the counselors of Orleans beseech him not to desert them in the hour of need; in vain the faithful Du Chatel offers him his life, which alone can reconcile the proud Burgundian,—the king remains firm in his resolve. But at the decisive moment the news comes that Baudricourt, with the help of a maiden, has won a brilliant victory. Soon thereafter, Johanna, whose whole demeanor reveals her divine mission, is led before the king, whom she recognizes, although she has never seen him; she knows of his nightly prayers, designates the place where the sword may be found which she is to carry, and foretells the death of the British general Salisbury and the deliverance of France. To explain her deeds she relates how the Virgin Mary appeared to her three nights in succession under an ancient oak at Dom Remy, and promised that she should destroy the enemy and lead the king to his coronation at Rheims, if she would renounce earthly love. Her appearance and her words inspire every one, and they give credence to her story.

Act II. Johanna has delivered Orleans and the enemy has fled;

but before the English can find rest in their hastily fortified camp, she climbs the ramparts, hurls fire into the camp, and fills the enemy with terror. She herself wields the sword in a fearful and merciless manner, slaying every one who steps in her way,—for the divine voice forbids her to show mercy. After this bloody victory she meets Philip of Burgundy, who is not kindly disposed toward the English, and wins him to her cause.

Act III. This act presents the tragic conflict. Johanna has thus far appeared to be free from human emotions; she rejects the offers of marriage made to her by the impetuous Dunois and the brave Lahire, and withstands the spectral black knight, who seeks to check her career. Faithful to her duty, she kills every living creature that the god of battle sends against her. The renunciation of human love is no sacrifice as long as she is not tempted; but when she overcomes the handsome young Englishman Lionel, and looks into his face, her sword falls from her hand, and her vow is broken.

Act IV. The coronation at Rheims becomes for Johanna the source of the most painful sorrow and deepest humiliation. Only under compulsion does she carry her banner at the head of the procession which conducts the king to the church. Among the people who have come to the celebration are the peasants of Dom Remy. When Johanna sees her sisters, the memory of home returns to her as a sweet comfort, and she yearns to cast all care and pomp aside and return with them to her home, to be again sister, daughter, and shepherdess. But before she can carry out her resolution, the king and his train come from the church, and suddenly, while the king hails her before all the people as the deliverer of France, her father steps out of the crowd and accuses her of being in league with the devil. Heaven itself seems to be against her, for heavy thunderclaps follow in rapid succession, and Johanna is filled with a sense of her guilt. The people scatter in all directions; the king, Lahire, and finally Dunois desert her; only Raimond, her faithful lover, accompanies her out of the city.

Act V. Johanna experiences her last humiliation in the hut of a charcoal burner, where even the cup is taken from her lips, because it is feared that misfortune will come from the "Witch of Orleans." She wanders about in the mountains until she falls into the hands of the English. But now she feels that her penitence has atoned for her guilt, and with the return of her old power she again devotes herself wholly to God. In reply to Isabeau's insults, as also to Lionel's proffered love, she has only this answer, "My people shall conquer, and I shall die." When the news of her capture reaches the French, whose warlike spirit has waned during her absence, they rush into the conflict anew to free her. As the battle rages she sinks to her knees and prays that her fetters may be broken; her prayer is answered, she wrests a sword from a soldier, and hastens into the thickest of the fray. Everything yields before her; the French army is rallied, the English flee, and Isabeau is captured, but Johanna dies on the field of battle, her face bright with the light from heaven.

DIE BRAUT VON MESSINA

Schiller became so enthusiastic over the works of Aeschylus and Sophocles that he also wished to try his hand at a tragedy in the antique form. Taking Sophocles' Oedipus as his model he selected the mediaeval city of Messina as the scene of his fate tragedy, which he called *Die Braut von Messina oder die feindlichen Brüder*. It was completed in January, 1803, and was the forerunner of the many fate tragedies which appeared in the next two decades. *Die Braut von Messina* is not divided into acts, but a chorus is introduced which furnishes a sort of commentary on what is to follow.

The Prince of Messina has brought a curse upon his house by marrying his father's bride. From early youth jealousy and hatred have existed between his two sons. This enmity, which their stern father alone could restrain, breaks out with renewed fury at his death. Don Manuel, the elder, is reserved and stern, the "better son," his mother Isabella, says; Don Caesar is frank and impulsive, and the real hero of the drama. Isabella finally succeeds in bringing about an interview between her two sons at which a reconciliation takes place, but she does not surmise that love for another has made their hearts more gentle. Don Caesar is, however, soon called away by the news that the maiden whose image he carries in his heart, but of whom he has lost all trace since their first meeting, has been discovered. Don Manuel rejoices in his brother's good fortune, for he also has a secret which he is about to disclose. He has fallen in love with a maiden whom he met some time before while hunting near the walls of a cloister. Her name is Beatrice, but she does not know who her parents are. She is now in Messina, where Don Manuel brought her when he learned that she was to be taken from the convent by her relatives. Isabella thinks this an opportune time to inform her sons that they have a sister who has grown up in a secret place, and is to-day to appear in the family circle for the first time. Beatrice, who was even at birth doomed to death by her father because an Arabian had warned him that she would cause the death of both her brothers, had been secretly conveyed by her mother to a convent, for her mother had had a dream, which a monk had interpreted favorably; that the daughter should unite the two hostile brothers in love. But the joy which so unexpectedly came to this sad house is short-lived. Beatrice has been carried away from the convent. Don Caesar wishes immediately to start in pursuit of the robbers, but Don Manuel, full of anxious foreboding, hastens to obtain further information.

Beatrice, meanwhile, has suffered hours of anxiety and expectation. While she is waiting for her lover, Don Caesar suddenly appears, and tells her that he intends to make her his bride; without waiting for her answer he hastens away and leaves his knights as guard. Beatrice can not rid herself of a consciousness of her guilt, for she had attended the funeral of the prince against the wishes of her lover, and there had met Don Caesar. When at last Don Manuel comes, Beatrice confesses her disobedience, and he sees through the whole pitiable affair; the brothers love the same maiden, and that maiden is their sister; but before he can make any explanation, Don Caesar appears and in blind jealousy kills his brother. The unconscious form of the maiden and the corpse of Don Manuel are brought to the unfortunate mother, who does not yet know who committed the crime. When Don Caesar himself confesses that he is the murderer, the mother is so overwhelmed with grief that she disowns him as her son; but she soon regrets this step, for she hears that he has resolved to remove the curse by his death. The thought of both sons in the grave is more terrible to her than the sight of the murderer, and so she recalls her curse and pleads with her despairing son; but just then the dirge from Don Manuel's grave comes as an admonition to avenge the death of the innocent one, and Don Caesar obeys the voice of Fate and stabs himself.

Wilhelm Tell

In this play Schiller strove to give a picture of the old Swiss people with all their peculiarities, in connection with a description of the country. Although Schiller had never seen Switzerland, he was able from his study of the country to portray accurately the Lake of Lucerne and its surroundings. His main purpose was, however, to show us the Forest Cantons of Switzerland,—Schwyz, Uri, and Unterwalden,—in the struggle against foreign conquerors. This drama, which Schiller based upon a Swiss chronicle of the sixteenth century by Aegidius Tschudi, was received with great applause in Weimar, where it was performed on March 17, 1804.

Act I. In this act we become acquainted with the conditions which bring about the Rütli Confederation. We learn how the peaceful peasants, who live with their families and their herds, are provoked to rebel; how the oppressor seeks to obtain their most sacred possessions; how the imperial governor, Gessler, to break their stubbornness, builds a fortress, called Zwing-Uri, at Altdorf, and erects a pole upon which is placed a hat, to which every one must pay homage with bended knee and bared head; and how Landenberg, the governor of Unterwalden, has the eyes of the old Heinrich von Melchthal put out because Arnold, his son, has escaped the revenge of the usurper by flight. In Uri, at the home of the honorable, cautious, but patriotic Walther Fürst, the plan for the liberation of the Forest Cantons is devised. Here the young, hot-tempered Arnold von Melchthal has taken refuge; to this place comes also Werner Stauffacher, "Father of the oppressed," a man of mature years, who has been sent by his noble wife, Gertrude, to arouse the people to throw off the yoke of oppression. They decide that each one of them shall in his respective canton win as many friends for the cause of liberty as possible, and that they shall then, each accompanied by ten trusty confederates, meet on a certain night on the Rütli. In this first act we are also introduced to Tell, a man of deeds, not words. He is best characterized in these words which he addresses to Stauffacher, "Yet, whatsoever you do, spare me from council; I was not born to deliberate and select; but when your course of action is resolved, then call on Tell; you shall not find him wanting."

ACT II. The Rütli scene occupies the greater part of this act. Among the thirty-three men who are assembled, both bond and free may be found; that Tell does not appear is not surprising. All agree that the governors and their servants must be driven out of the country, and the fortified castles destroyed,—if possible without bloodshed. The only difference of opinion seems to be whether they shall rise up in arms immediately, or wait until a later day; the latter opinion prevails, and Christmas is chosen as the time for vengeance. The old Baron von Attinghausen is the only Swiss nobleman who is in sympathy with the peasants. Ulrich von Rudenz, his young nephew, is attracted to the Austrian court by his love for Bertha von Bruneck.

ACT III. While out on a hunt, Rudenz learns from Bertha that he has misunderstood her. She confesses that she has associated with Gessler only because her Austrian relatives intrusted her to him, but that her sympathies are with the Forest Cantons, in which her possessions are situated. If he wishes to marry her, he must make himself worthy of her love by assisting in the deliverance of his Fatherland. These words arouse his patriotic feelings and he soon finds an opportunity to show his colors. Because Tell has refused to bow before the hat, he is condemned to shoot an apple from the head of his young son, Walther, in the market place at Altdorf. The apple falls and the boy is uninjured. Tell has been seen to conceal a second arrow in his doublet, which he fearlessly confesses was intended for the tyrant had the first one injured his boy.

Act IV. To rid himself of this dangerous enemy, the governor has Tell bound and taken to a boat which is to take him to a dungeon at Küssnacht. While they are crossing the lake a fearful storm arises, and Tell is unbound to steer the boat, but he escapes by leaping out upon a projecting ledge of rock. He hastens on to the "hohle Gasse" where he awaits the tyrant and sends an arrow through his heart. Tell considers this a sacred duty which he owes to his family and his country, as well as the fulfillment of a vow made when he was forced to aim at the head of his child. Meanwhile the faithful old Baron von Attinghausen dies and at his deathbed Rudenz confesses his error, pledges his support to the patriots, and implores their assistance in the liberation of Bertha, whom Gessler has had secretly abducted.

Act V. Tell's deed arouses the people to set about the work of liberation at once. The cantons rise in force and overthrow the strongholds of tyranny, Landenberg flees never to return, and the emperor, Albrecht, is assassinated by his nephew, Johann von Schwaben.

Tell turns the parricide from his door, disclaiming all similarity between their deeds, and shows him the way to Rome, where he is to confess his crime to the pope. The drama closes with a great gathering of the confederates to thank Tell for what he has done for his country and the betrothal of Rudenz and Bertha.

Johann Wolfgang von Goethe (1749–1832)

The greatest man in the history of German literature is Johann Wolfgang von Goethe, who was born at Frankfort on the Main, August 28, 1749. His father, who bore the title of Imperial Counselor, was

married at the age of thirty-eight to Katharina
Elizabeth, the seventeen-year old daughter of Johann
Wolfgang Textor, the chief magistrate of the city.
Goethe's father was quite wealthy and well educated, and had traveled considerably in Germany and
Italy. Being pedantic and despotic in disposition,
he was not greatly loved, but was always respected
for his upright character. He also manifested great
interest in art and literature and wished to give his
son every opportunity possible for intellectual development and culture. Goethe's mother was affable,
genial, full of good humor, and yet dignified and refined in her tastes. She was the sympathetic companion of her son and shared his joys and sorrows;
she called him her "hätschel Hans" and told him
stories which aroused his youthful fancy; and when
he became famous she was proud of his achievements
and entertained his friends. What he inherited from
his parents he tells in these lines:

> "Vom Vater hab' ich die Statur,
>   Des Lebens ernstes Führen;
>   Vom Mütterchen die Frohnatur,
>   Die Lust zu fabulieren."

Goethe was a very precocious child, who early
was surrounded by intellectual influences, and never
knew adversity as did Schiller. He and his sister,
Cornelia, developed a love for literature and became
intimate companions in every department of their
youthful activity. In his autobiography, *Dichtung*

und Wahrheit, Goethe gives a full and interesting account of his childhood and youth, closing with the events of 1775. Before he was twelve years old he began to write verses and fantastic tales, and laid the foundation for future studies. The old city of Frankfort, a marionette theater, the Seven Years' War, the occupation of the city by French soldiers and the performances of French theatrical troupes made deep and lasting impressions on the boy's mind, and served to develop that independence and self-reliance which characterized him later in life. His first love episode occurred in 1764 with Gretchen, a Frankfort girl, but it was of short duration. In 1765, Goethe was sent to the University of Leipzig to study law. Leipzig, the "little Paris" of Germany, was quite metropolitan and offered the provincial student many opportunities of learning and culture. French influence was dominant in society and Goethe was soon imbued with its spirit. Gellert was enjoying literary fame, and greatly influenced Goethe's prose style; Gottsched, once recognized as a leader in literature, was on the decline. Like Lessing, who also studied here, Goethe found the theater the chief source of attraction, and considered the lectures of the professors dry and uninteresting. He preferred to write love songs for the composer Breitkopf, and took considerable interest in art and engraving. His love for Anna Katharina Schönkopf, a coquettish maiden of nineteen, at whose home he dined, gave

him the experience which we find embodied in the
"Schäferspiel," *Die Laune des Verliebten*, written in
1767–68. His second drama, *Die Mitschuldigen*, is
also a product of this period and shows Goethe's
realistic tendencies. His letters to his relatives and
friends give us the best history of his student life here.
The three years in Leipzig were wasted by society,
neglect of study, and a disappointing love affair, and,
attacked by a hemorrhage of the lungs, he was obliged
to return home. After he recovered, his father proposed that he should complete his studies in Strassburg, and on the 2d of April, 1770, he reached the
city where his literary aspirations were to be stimulated and his genius discovered. A new circle of
congenial acquaintances was soon formed, to which
belonged Jung-Stilling, a part of whose autobiography, *Heinrich Stillings Jugend*, Goethe published
in 1777. The most influential of his new friends was
Herder, already an author of great reputation, and a
critic second only to Lessing. He stimulated Goethe
to poetic activity, called his attention to the beauties
of Gothic architecture, and showed him the wealth of
charm and beauty in the folk poetry and literature of
other nations. Weyland, a fellow-student, took him
in the autumn of 1770 to Sesenheim in Alsace, and
introduced him to the family of pastor Brion. Here
Goethe met Friederike, a gentle, graceful, simple,
and lady-like girl with blue eyes and slender figure,
and soon "the most charming idyl in the history of

modern literature" developed. The beautiful lyrics which this innocent girl inspired gave Goethe a place by the side of Walther von der Vogelweide as a lyric poet. But before many months had passed Goethe discovered the great difference in their stations in life, and a separation took place which broke the heart of the confiding maiden and filled Goethe's heart with sorrow and despair. Friederike never married, and when Goethe visited her eight years afterward she was unchanged and treated him with the greatest courtesy. She died in 1813. In August, 1771, Goethe received the degree of licentiate of law and returned to Frankfort. The legal profession did not attract him as much as the ideals of the *Sturm und Drang*, the struggle against the shallow pettiness of social and political conditions and all conventional restraints, the right to enjoy life in all its fullness. In the spring of 1772 Goethe made repeated excursions to Darmstadt, where he met Herder's fiancée, Caroline Flachsland, and J. H. Merck, a man of good common sense who exerted a restraining influence on the young, enthusiastic poet. In May of the same year Goethe went to Wetzlar, the seat of the imperial law courts, to prepare himself better for his profession; but again he fell in love and only through a terrible inner struggle was he able to save himself from suicide. Charlotte Buff, the daughter of the magistrate, was engaged to a young jurist named Kestner, whose friendship Goethe had won. Goethe's love for Lotte soon became a passion, and a crisis was impending; a sudden departure, a visit to Frau Sophie von Laroche, and a trip up the Rhine dampened his ardor, and the result of the episode was *Werther*. He soon regained his equilibrium and found healing for his grief in zealous devotion to literary work. His greatest achievement during this period, and the work which made him suddenly the greatest writer in Germany, was *Götz von Berlichingen*.

Götz von Berlichingen

In Götz, the man with the iron hand, Goethe pictures the life of an independent knight at the time of the Reformation, to whom "might is right." Goethe found that the conditions of the time in which he lived corresponded in many respects with those described in Götz's autobiography; consequently the play appealed strongly to his own contemporaries, and when it appeared in 1773, it was greeted by a storm of applause. As the first successful historical drama, *Götz* marks the beginning of a new epoch in German literature.

Act I. Götz lives in his castle at Jaxthausen. His household consists of his wife Elizabeth, a brave, intrepid woman, his sister Maria, and his little son Karl. He possesses all the good and the bad qualities of a knight of the empire. He is brave and honest, and his word is equal to an oath; his greatest treasure is liberty, his favorite occupation warfare. When his right hand was shot off, he had an iron one made, and learned to wield his sword with his left hand. His greatest enemy is the bishop of Bamberg, a vain, deceitful man, who, notwithstanding his agreement with Götz, has captured one of his men. This gives rise to a new feud, in which Weislingen, Götz's playmate at school, but now the bishop's stanchest supporter, is taken prisoner. Götz's kindly treatment of his old friend wins his heart; he is betrothed to Maria, and promises, neither publicly nor privately to assist the enemies of Götz. But Götz underestimates the weakness of his friend, who is both fickle and cowardly. At the court he is better known, for "no Weislingen can tear himself away from the handshake of a prince nor from the smile of a beautiful woman!"

Act II. Weislingen returns to Bamberg to put his affairs in order, and soon yields to the allurements of court life; he forgets Maria and his promise to Götz, and marries the heartless and coquettish Adelheid von Walldorf. He is even willing to go to Augsburg to induce the emperor to take steps against Götz and his followers.

Act III. Götz is now declared an outlaw, and the imperial troops set out to destroy Jaxthausen and kill or capture the inhabitants. This proves to be a difficult task, for Götz has many friends who are willing to risk life and limb for him. Franz von Sickingen sends him reënforcements, and also relieves him of all care concerning his sister by seeking her hand in marriage. The soldiers are repeatedly repulsed before they are able to surround Jaxthausen, and when they finally succeed, their loss is so great that they declare their willingness to allow the prisoners to withdraw. But hardly have Götz and his people passed through the gate when they are treacherously attacked and overpowered; some of the bravest are killed, others are thrown into the tower, and Götz himself is committed to the tower at Heilbronn to await his fate.

Act IV. The emperor decrees that Götz must remain at Heilbronn and take oath that he will in no way take revenge on any of his enemies. Götz is willing to submit to these conditions, but when he seeks to learn the whereabouts of his men before taking his oath, the councilors declare him a rebel, and seek to have him cast into the dungeon. In this extremity Franz von Sickingen appears with two hundred horsemen, and threatens to set fire to the four corners of the city if any injury is done to Götz. Forced by the superior numbers of the enemy the councilors allow their prisoner to withdraw to his castle on condition that he will remain inactive.

Act V. The idleness to which Götz finds himself condemned is for him the greatest punishment. He, however, keeps his promise until the rebellious peasants, who everywhere have risen up against their lords, and have overrun the country, murdering, plundering, and burning, compel him to become their leader. Götz hopes to be of service to the empire by restraining the rebels, but he is disappointed; they will not obey him. It becomes an easy matter for Weislingen, who arrives with a strong force, to annihilate the peasants. Götz is wounded in the conflict, taken captive, and thrown into the tower at Heilbronn, where he is condemned to death. His fate is in the hands of Weislingen, who himself lies ill in his castle; his ambitious wife, Adelheid, has had him poisoned because he stood in the way of her plans. Maria comes to the bedside of the dying man to seek her brother's release; this is granted, but Götz can not enjoy his renewed freedom, for he, too, is nigh unto death. The circumstances of which he has been a victim have robbed him of his strength; while seeking rest and change in the prison garden he breathes his last in the arms of his faithful wife, with the words, "Es lebe die Freiheit!" upon his lips. Adelheid is convicted of murder and adultery, and condemned to death by the Holy Vehm.

Goethe's attachment to Charlotte Buff furnished the material for his romance *Die Leiden des jungen Werthers*, which appeared in the autumn of 1774 and became exceedingly popular. It was suited to the morbid sentimentality of the age, and the "Werther fever" soon spread all over Europe. Johann Lavater's name was added to the coterie of Goethe's friends in the eventful year 1774. Lavater was a pastor in Zürich, who entertained individualistic ideas on religion and advocated the so-called science of physiognomy. At first Goethe was inclined to share Lavater's hallucinations, but in time the latter's religious sentimentality became repugnant to him. Another friend who influenced Goethe was F. H. Jacobi, of Düsseldorf, a more congenial but less brilliant man than Lavater. He was imbued with the spirit of Wertherism and succeeded in directing Goethe's attention to Spinoza's philosophy. The beginning of the year 1775 finds the poet again involved in a love affair with Lili Schönemann, the daughter of a rich banker in Frankfort. Her girlish näiveté and coquettishness beguiled him into her snares, and an engagement, which was afterward broken, resulted. A trip to Switzerland with the two brothers Stolberg cured him of the idea that he could not exist without Lili. Many of his most beautiful lyrics were called forth by this attachment and evince his strong passion and self-control.

The rapidly increasing fame of the young author attracted the attention of Duke Karl August of Weimar, a man of literary tastes, who invited him to spend a few weeks at his court. Goethe was so well pleased with his reception that he decided to take up his residence there in 1775, and soon became the bosom friend of the duke and later his prime minister, a position which he held until within a few years of his death. In the interval between his return from Strassburg and his removal to Weimar, Goethe produced the dramatic satires *Götter, Helden und Wieland, Hanswursts Hochzeit, Pater Brey, Satyros,* and *Das Jahrmarktsfest zu Plundersweilern.* Two burgher dramas, *Clavigo* (1774) and *Stella* (1776), after the style of Lessing's *Emilia Galotti,* and two "Singspiele," *Erwin und Elmire* (1775) and *Claudine von Villa Bella* (1776), also appeared. The tragedies *Sokrates* and *Mahomet,* the one philosophical in character, and the other religious, the epic *Der ewige Jude* and the drama *Prometheus* remain as fragments of this period. Shortly after Goethe's arrival in Weimar he met Charlotte von Stein, the first lady of noble birth with whom he became intimately acquainted. Though she was seven years older than he, and the mother of seven children, an intimacy developed between them which lasted until 1786, and produced a long series of "the most beautiful love letters that ever flowed from the pen of man." She, of all the women whom he loved, influenced him most, and taught him self-control and resignation. This first decade of Weimar life was productive of the most beautiful lyrics Goethe has written, and reveal his happiness in his new love and his high appreciation of nature. The *Harzreise im Winter* was made in 1777, and a second Swiss journey with the duke in 1779. Returning, they stopped at Stuttgart to visit the Karlsschule, where Schiller was a student. The next year appeared another "Singspiel," *Jery und Bätely,* and that excellent poem *Gesang der Geister über den Wassern.* Plans for *Egmont, Tasso,* and *Wilhelm Meister*, and the completion of *Iphigenie* date back to this period. In 1786, Goethe carried out his long-cherished plan of a journey to Italy, where he remained two years. Here his views of life were changed, his vision was enlarged and his ideals of art and poetry matured; *Iphigenie* was also re-written in its present form, *Egmont* was completed, and on the way home in 1788 he worked at *Tasso* which was finished in 1789. His experiences in Italy, gleaned from his letters and diaries at a later time, are to be found in the volume of his works under the title *Italienische Reise* (1786–88). Goethe was an entirely different man when he returned from Italy. He seemed estranged from his former friends, and did not wish to be burdened with any duties other than the supervision of the University of Jena and the Court Theater.

IPHIGENIE AUF TAURIS

This drama with its calm grandeur and smooth versification is almost faultless in artistic style. The material is borrowed from the Greek. But while the heroine of Euripides' tragedy is characterized by cunning and sagacity, which is the inheritance of her people, Goethe's Iphigenie is incapable of deceit; she is the representative of true womanhood, the incorporation of moral strength. In the Greek tragedy the conflict can be solved only by the intervention of a deity; in the German all the difficulties are adjusted by the moral force of the heroine.

The play was first written in prose in 1779 and re-written in its present form while the poet was in Italy in 1787. It was acted for the first time in the duke's private theater in Weimar and is considered the most psychological of all of Goethe's works.

ACT I. Iphigenie, the daughter of Agamemnon, had been carried to Tauris by the goddess Artemis, when her father was about to sacrifice her to appease the wrath of the gods. She has already spent many years far from her home. As priestess she is honored by the people, and has succeeded in revoking the old custom of human sacrifice, and yet she is not happy; she can not repress her longing for her home. "Weh' dem, der fern von Eltern und Geschwistern ein einsam Leben führt." As she sadly wanders through the grove of the temple, Arkas, the intimate friend of King Thoas, comes to her and bids her prepare to meet his master, who intends to demand her hand in marriage. Iphigenie trusts to the good sense of the king and to her own powers of persuasion to avert the catastrophe, which would forever prevent her return to her people. She reveals to Thoas that she is of the accursed race of Tantalus; but the king persists in his demand. When she remains firm, Thoas declares that she shall remain priestess, but that from this time forth every stranger, who comes to the shores of Tauris must be sacrificed according to ancient custom. Two strangers who are concealed in the caverns on the shore are to be the first victims.

ACT II. The two strangers are Iphigenie's brother, Orestes, and his friend Pylades. Agamemnon has been slain by his wife, Klytemnestra, and Aegisthus; Orestes avenges his father's death by killing his mother and her paramour. To escape from the Furies who are pursuing him, he consults Apollo, who declares that the curse will be removed if Orestes can bring back to Greece his sister who tarries in Tauris against her will. The unfortunate man believes it to be Apollo's own sister whom he is to rescue

from the barbarians, and he sets out in a ship with his friend
Pylades. When they reach the inhospitable Scythian shore, and
find themselves in great danger, Pylades is full of life and courage,
and thinks only of their deliverance; Orestes is melancholy, and
longs for death. Now for the first time since her miraculous rescue,
Iphigenie meets a Greek, and it is but natural that the desire to
hear from her loved ones is uppermost in her mind. They meet
without recognizing one another, and Pylades tells her of the great
events of the Trojan war, and of the tragic fate of her father.

Act III. Orestes does not wish to deceive the priestess as did
Pylades, who said they were the sons of the king of Crete, but reveals himself to her, and confesses his guilt. Iphigenie now makes
herself known to them. When Orestes learns that he is destined
to die by her hand, he sinks overcome to the ground. Recovering
from his swoon he believes himself in the lower world living in
peace with his ancestors. Thus Iphigenie and Pylades find him.
The climax of the drama is reached when the pure and sanctify-
ing presence of his sister frees Orestes from the fetters of the curse,
and the Furies leave him. It now remains for the three to make
good their escape with the image of the goddess.

Act IV. While Orestes and Pylades seek their companions on
the shore, Iphigenie, according to Pylades' plan, is to inform the
king that the temple has been desecrated by the presence of a
matricide, and that the image of the goddess needs purification in
the waves of the sea. They can then make their way to a vessel
concealed on the coast and carry the image away. When Arkas
calls Iphigenie to account for the delay in offering the sacrifice she
takes refuge in deceit. But the consciousness of the twofold guilt
of deceiving the king and stealing the image torments her pure
soul, and even Pylades can not overcome her scruples.

Act V. The conduct of the priestess and the prisoners arouses
the suspicions of the Taurians, and Thoas commands Iphigenie
to appear before him. Neither the king nor the priestess is an
adept at misrepresentation. Even after having allowed herself
to be persuaded by Pylades to deceive the king, Iphigenie can not
at the critical moment tell him a lie. She confides in the great soul
of the ruler who has been so kind to her, and tells him the whole
truth, pleading that she may be allowed to return peaceably with

her brother and his friend to her own home. Her confidence has not been misplaced; Thoas listens to the voice of humanity and grants her request. But at this moment the appearance of Orestes at the head of armed Greeks threatens to destroy all that Iphigenie has gained. Orestes, however, also has lofty ideals, and voluntarily gives up the image, perceiving now that he has found the solution of the oracle in the rescue of his own sister. The king graciously permits them to depart, and extends his hand to Iphigenie with a word of farewell.

EGMONT

Goethe found in Count Egmont a hero like Götz von Berlichingen. As Götz was a representative of knighthood at the time of the Reformation, so Egmont is a true type of the Dutch nobility at the time when the fate of Flanders had reached a critical point. Although the poet's presentation is not always true to history, he nevertheless depicts very clearly the persons and conditions of which Egmont is the center of attraction. Goethe began to write *Egmont* as early as 1775, but it was not completed until the summer of 1787. Like *Götz*, it is written in prose.

ACT I. At a meeting of the archers in the city of Brussels the conversation centers on Count Egmont, the governor of Artois and Flanders, the victor of St. Quentin and Gravelingen. Although he does not himself appear in this act, we nevertheless become acquainted with his character. All agree that he is generous, open-hearted, and brave; all feel oppressed by the Spanish rule, and especially by the Spanish Inquisition, and see in Egmont their natural protector. The picture of the hero is made complete by the interview which the regent of the Netherlands, Margarete von Parma, sister of King Philip II., has in her palace with her private secretary, Machiavell. She discovers in Egmont's popularity the greatest danger to her rule, for the people notice the difference between his cheerful, indifferent conduct, and the severity of Philip's government. She is also personally offended by the independent attitude of the count, who acts as if he were not a subject of the king, but were himself lord of the Netherlands. And yet she is obliged to admit that he is conscientious in everything, and that he has never concealed his ambition.

ACT II. Egmont's conduct confirms the opinion which the people and the court have of him. The manner in which he calms the citizens who have been aroused by Secretary Vansen shows how much the people love him. A letter from a well-meaning friend, who warns him to be more careful, leads him to a self-examination which unveils his innermost heart; he believes that the hope of the enjoyment of life makes life worth living; he is ambitious to be more than he is, but does not wish to weigh carefully the importance of every step. He pays no attention to the warnings of his friend, William of Orange, whose character is just the opposite of his own. Silent and cautious, Orange seeks to know the opinion of others, and to discover the plans of his enemies in order to defeat them. He has learned that the blood-thirsty Duke of Alba is coming to the Netherlands with an army, and he is convinced that Margarete will abdicate rather than maintain a semblance of the power which is actually in the hands of another. He therefore decides to leave Brussels, never to return as long as Alba continues to rule. Egmont can not understand such conduct; he trusts in his own right, in the justice of the king, and in the wisdom of the imperial councilors. Consequently Orange can not persuade him to flee from the threatened danger.

ACT III. What Orange surmised now becomes a reality; Margarete secretly leaves Brussels. While the heavy clouds are collecting over Egmont's head he spends his days in unconcern. Klärchen, his little sweetheart, almost worships him, and the last cloud which his friend's departure has brought over him disappears in her presence.

ACT IV. The king has sent Alba into the provinces not only to restore order temporarily, but also to deprive the individual states of their liberty, and thus once for all to destroy the opposition.

Alba is the very man to carry out this plan. He knows not the enjoyments of life; accustomed from his youth up to obey and to command, he does not understand the need of individual liberty. He steadfastly goes about his work, and resolves first of all to capture the leading nobles, especially Egmont and Orange, and render them forever harmless. Under pretense of seeking their advice he invites them to his castle. Orange sends a letter from Antwerp in which he excuses his absence, but Egmont unsuspectingly goes into the trap which is set for him; upon a spirited horse, as if he were going to a great feast, he gallops into the courtyard, and with a feeling of quiet security enters the room. When he learns that the people are to be deprived of their freedom he declares that they would rather die than be robbed of their rights. Expressing the hope that all may yet be well, Egmont seeks to take his leave, but the gallery is occupied by guards and he is obliged to surrender.

ACT V. When Klärchen hears what has happened, she hastens in the twilight through the streets of Brussels, accompanied by her faithful yet hopeless lover, Brackenburg, to arouse the citizens to free Egmont. But no one has the courage to risk his life in the attempt, and crushed in spirit she returns to her home. Soon afterward Brackenburg informs her that a scaffold is being erected on the market place, and that Egmont, without doubt, will die on the following morning. Klärchen then takes poison. Meanwhile the sentence of death is read to Egmont in the prison. At first he is filled with resentment at the injustice done him, for, as a Knight of the Golden Fleece, he can be condemned only by the Grand Master of that order, together with the assembled chapter of knights. When, however, Ferdinand, the young son of Alba, who is present when the verdict is read, reminds him of his earlier life, which the youth of the land have sought to imitate, his old heroism returns and he resolves that his death shall also be worthy of imitation. After Ferdinand has gone, a gentle slumber comes over the prisoner and a pleasant dream seems to bear his spirit away; the goddess of liberty, who has the features of Klärchen, extends to him a laurel wreath, and announces to him that his death will secure freedom for the Netherlands. The dream still lingers after he has awakened. The drums which summon him to death seem to him the signal of victory, and as he advances through the guards he cries out: "Protect your homes! And to save those who are most dear to you, be ready to follow my example, and fall with joy!"

TASSO

This psychological drama, first written in prose 1780–81, but rewritten in blank verse while the poet was in Italy, was published in 1790. Although wanting in dramatic action, it is superior to *Iphigenie* in delicate poetic charm and fine delineation of character. The life of Torquato Tasso, author of *La Gerusalemme Liberata*, who died in Rome in 1595, combined with Goethe's own experiences in Weimar, furnished the material for this work.

ACT I. Tasso comes to the court of the Duke Alphonso II., of Ferrara, where he expects to find time and inspiration to complete his poem, *Jerusalem Delivered*. He is encouraged in his work by his love for the duke's sister, Leonore von Este, and from her conversation with the Countess Leonore Sanvitale in the garden of the castle Belriguardo, we learn that she secretly returns his love. Notwithstanding the similarity of these two women in education and intellectual interests they differ greatly in character. The princess is tall and delicate, of reserved and melancholy disposition, but always kind and unselfish; the countess, on the other hand, is small of stature, delights in the pleasures of life, and is not without deceit and selfishness; essentially a "lighter being," but one of the poet's most charming creations. The conversation of the two friends is interrupted by the entrance of the duke. He is seeking Tasso, who, he believes, spends too much time in seclusion. When the duke invited him to his court he doubtless thought only of the fame of his house, and he still believes that the world will be indebted to Ferrara for this noble work. He is, nevertheless, generous enough to consider the welfare of his *protégé*, and when he urges him to finish the poem, he does so in order to introduce him as soon as possible to the world, so that he may develop his character. Tasso lacks the qualities which would enable him to live and work before the public; he is suspicious and excitable, sensitive and passionate, and his idealism can not adjust itself to the stern realities of life. Thus we find him when he has completed his work, and modestly comes to present it to the duke. When the princess, at the wish of the duke, takes a laurel wreath from the bust of Virgil and places it upon Tasso's head, he imagines himself in Elysium, at the side of Homer and the heroes of antiquity, but he is soon to realize that he is yet in the world of realities. Antonio, the Secretary of State, has just returned from Rome, and informs the duke of the successful turn in his affairs. The honor conferred upon the inexperienced poet displeases the shrewd, practical statesman, arouses his jealousy, and a quarrel between the two men so differently constituted is inevitable.

ACT II. Tasso, deeply wounded by Antonio's disparaging remarks, is consoled by the princess, who confesses that she is pleased with his verses, but demands of him moderation and renunciation. At her desire he seeks a reconciliation with Antonio and impetuously offers him his friendship, which the man of the world coldly rejects. The breach continues to widen until Tasso, bitterly offended, draws his sword. Just then the duke appears, and mildly punishes the poet by banishing him to his room for an indefinite period. He also censures Antonio, who, as the more experienced man, should have exercised greater indulgence, and subsequently commands him to become reconciled with the poet, and to give him his liberty.

ACT III. In this act Tasso remains in the background, and the intrigue of Countess Sanvitale is disclosed. She proposes as the best solution of the trouble that Tasso should leave Ferrara for a while, and accompany her to Florence, where she hopes to captivate him and make him an ornament for herself. This plan does not find favor with the princess, who wishes to keep Tasso near her, nor with Antonio, who would not have it seem that he is the cause of the poet's departure.

ACT IV. Tasso's morbid condition of mind develops into the delusion that all his former friends are plotting to get him out of Ferrara, and he becomes unjust and deceitful. In compliance with the duke's command Antonio seeks to make his peace with Tasso, and bids him put his friendship to the test. Tasso requests Antonio to obtain the duke's permission for him to leave Ferrara that he may go to Rome, and there, with the help of his friends, give his poem the finishing touches. Antonio tries to persuade him to remain, but at last reluctantly consents to speak to the duke.

Act V. The duke very unwillingly gives his consent, and bids the poet a cordial farewell, expressing the hope that he will soon return. The appearance of the princess dispels Tasso's suspicions, and he is conscious only of the approaching separation. When she speaks kindly to him, and reproaches him for wishing to leave his friends, his strength utterly forsakes him, and unmindful of the entrance of the duke and Antonio, he makes a frenzied declaration of love and presses the princess to his bosom. Throwing him from her she hastily retires. By this presumptuous act Tasso himself inevitably severs the tie that binds him to the court. Forsaken on every side he finds in Antonio at last a noble friend and comforter.

To the year 1790 belong *Faust, ein Fragment,* and the *Venetianischen Epigramme,* which were followed in 1794 by a translation of the Low German beast Epic *Reineke Fuchs* and the *Römischen Elegien* in 1795. Goethe was also to taste life on the battlefield, and accompanied the duke in the campaign against the French, an account of which he gives in *Campagne in Frankreich,* 1792, but not published until 1822. His intimate acquaintance with Schiller was a notable factor in the great poet's life. Notwithstanding the failure of the previous attempts to bring the two gifted men together, a meeting in Jena during the summer of 1794 was more successful. From now on they became fast friends and were mutually helpful.

Goethe became a contributor to Schiller's magazines, *Die Horen* and *Musenalmanach*, exchanged ideas and literary plans, and assisted in the publication of short satirical thrusts at their enemies, called *Xenien*. This friendship continued until the death of Schiller in 1805. Goethe's romance *Wilhelm Meisters Lehrjahre*, which consists of six books, appeared in 1795–96, and was the pioneer of the autobiographical German novel. It relates the experiences of a young man who, contrary to the wishes of his father, becomes an actor, joins a theatrical troupe, and then finds that he has missed his calling. This romance, which includes some beautiful poems like *Mignon*, and the work *Bekenntnisse einer schönen Seele*, shows Goethe's enlarged views of life and depicts the state of German society of that age.

After the rupture with Frau von Stein Goethe transferred his affections to Christiane Vulpius, an attractive, intelligent, and affectionate girl, whom he took into his house as his mistress, but whom he did not marry until 1806. This love affair caused considerable scandal in Weimar society and made Goethe many enemies. In the year 1797 Goethe vied with Schiller in writing ballads for the *Musenalmanach*, and in the next year *Hermann und Dorothea* appeared.

HERMANN UND DOROTHEA

This poem, which is composed of nine cantos, each of which bears the name of a muse, is one of Goethe's best productions, and may be styled an epic-idyl. Goethe found his material in the story of the fugitive Protestants whom the Archbishop of Salzburg expelled from his territory in 1731; but the poet transferred the time of action to his own age, and in place of the Salzburg exiles he presents to us German emigrants who have been driven from their homes by marauding French soldiers. It is written in hexameters, the characters are few and clearly drawn, and the whole is characterized by simplicity of style and subject. It gives us a beautiful picture of simple domestic life in a small German town, interwoven with events arising from the French Revolution. Its patriotic spirit appealed to the public and it soon gained a wide popularity.

The scene of this charming epic is thought by some to be Pössneck in Thuringia, by others, some village along the Rhine. The streets seem deserted, for most of the inhabitants have gone out to the chaussée to see the arriving emigrants. Hermann, the son of the host of the "Golden Lion," has also driven out to bring the fugitives food and linen. His parents are anxiously awaiting his return at the doorway of their house. His father, though grieved by the story of want and distress, comforts himself with the thought of his own prosperity; his mother is a typical German housewife and is tactful in adjusting the differences which often arise between father and son. They have not waited long when some of the villagers, including the loquacious apothecary and the noble pastor, return covered with dust, and relate their experiences. When Hermann comes home, he tells how he overtook a brave young maiden guiding an ox cart in which lay a woman with her newborn babe; and how he gave her the food and clothing his mother had sent, believing that she would distribute them wisely among the sick and needy. Hermann is tall and well grown, modest and respectful in manner, but lacking in ambition and enterprise, and too diffident to please his father, who wishes him to court their rich neighbor's daughter. The pastor remarks that he has never seen Hermann so cheerful before; for the quiet, reserved youth, accustomed only to obey, has suddenly developed firmness and determination of character, and seems no longer unwilling to think of marriage. When the wary and timid apothecary congratulates himself that he has no family for which to provide in these troublous days, Hermann earnestly protests, and says that many a good maiden needs a husband now to protect her. His father warns him that he will accept none but a rich maiden as a daughter; this comes as a blow to the young man, and he leaves the room, followed by his kind mother, to whom he confides that he loves the emigrant girl and is determined to make her his wife. The mother returns and informs her husband and his friends of Hermann's determination to marry the exiled maiden. The pastor takes his part, but the more cautious apothecary suggests that inquiries should first be made about Dorothea. The father reluctantly gives his consent, and the pastor and the apothecary, accompanied by Hermann, go to the neighboring village where the emigrants are stopping, to learn what reputation the maiden bears among her own people. Hermann's good opinion of the girl is confirmed. The character of this capable, self-denying maiden has been developed by sad experiences, since both her parents and her lover have been taken from her by death. Hermann meets her at the well, where she has come to draw water, but he can not bring himself to speak to her of love; he tells her instead that his mother is in need of a strong, reliable maiden to help her in the house. The homeless girl, believing herself engaged as a servant, bids her friends farewell, and gladly accompanies Hermann to his home. Before he has time, however, to explain his conduct, the father, believing that she knows all, offends her by expressing his admiration of her beauty, and his approval of his son's choice. She thus feels herself placed in a false position, and resolves to leave the house at once. But the wise pastor adroitly makes use of this opportunity to win from the maiden the confession that her feeling for the excellent young man is deeper than gratitude, and that she has secretly hoped that she may some day be deemed worthy of becoming his bride; but she now realizes that the difference between the rich youth and the poor exile is indeed too great, and she begs to be allowed to return to her people. When Hermann hears this he no longer conceals his feelings; Dorothea is made acquainted with the real position she is expected to fill in the household, and a betrothal follows. The charming maiden pays a beautiful tribute to the memory of her former lover, and the poem concludes, as it opened, with a reference to national events.

During the next ten years Goethe's activity was limited to a few "Festspiele," like *Was wir bringen* and *Paläophron und Neoterpe*, the historical tragedy *Die Natürliche Tochter*, writings on art, and a few minor works like *Der Gross-Cophta*, *Der Bürgergeneral*, and *Pandora*.

How deeply Goethe was moved by the death of Schiller may be learned from his magnificent *Epilog zu Schillers Glocke*. After a vain attempt to complete his friend's unfinished tragedy *Demetrius*, his muse slumbered for some time, and all literary efforts seemed suspended until 1808, when the First Part of *Faust* was published.

The popularity of *Faust* stimulated Goethe to renewed endeavors, and in 1809 *Die Wahlverwandtschaften*, the first important work in the last period of the poet's life, appeared. Reflections on his love for Minna Herzlieb of Jena furnished the theme for this psychological novel, which treats of the moral problems of marriage. Although sixty years of age, Goethe's genius had not declined, of which vivacious drinking songs and ballads like *Johanna Sebus* and *Der getreue Eckart* give evidence. As in his earlier years, so now in 1810 he showed his scientific turn of mind by writing the *Farbenlehre* and *Zur Morphologie*. In the following year he published the first volume of his autobiography under the title *Aus meinem Leben: Dichtung und Wahrheit;* the second and third volumes were finished by the end of 1814, but the fourth did not appear until after his death.

During the last years of his life Goethe withdrew more and more from active public life, and he was not at all interested in the War of Liberation. But when the victory was won he rejoiced with his people in the new spirit which seemed to animate the national consciousness, and then wrote *Des Epimenides Erwachen* in 1814. About this time a translation of the Persian poet Hafis fell into Goethe's hands and he took up the study of oriental poetry. The result of this study was a collection of love songs inspired by his love for Marianne von Willemer, and published in the year 1819 under the title *Der Westöstliche Divan.* These lyrics betray the effects of approaching age and are more reflective than his earlier poems. *Wilhelm Meisters Wanderjahre*, a part of which appeared in 1821, but which was not completed until 1829, is not comparable as a piece of fiction with the *Lehrjahre*. It deals with similar social problems, but the individual no longer tries to assert himself against society; he seeks rather to adjust himself to his environment and to make himself useful.

The last years of the poet's life are full of interesting experiences. He sought to keep himself abreast of the time and did not allow old age to rob him of his vitality and usefulness. He realized that the age was changing and that he must adapt himself to it. Among the frequent visitors at the court was Bettina Brentano, with whom Goethe became intimately acquainted in the Werther days, and who wrote *Goethes Briefwechsel mit einem Kinde.* Napoleon, Beethoven, Scott, Byron, Carlyle, Eckermann, von Humboldt, and a host of other friends cheered him by expressions of admiration and appreciation. Wieland died in 1813, and in 1816 Goethe was grieved by the loss of his wife; the following year he gave up the directorship of the theater, the duties of which had become too burdensome for him. But he was not yet too old to love, for even in his seventy-fourth year he became passionately fond of Ulrike von Levetzow, a girl of nineteen, whom he met at Marienbad in the summer of 1822. The beautiful *Marienbader Elegie* and the *Trilogie der Leidenschaft* remain as tokens of this love and consequent suffering. Meanwhile his sorrows were multiplied by the death of many of his old friends, among them Charlotte von Stein in 1827, and in the following year Duke Karl August. To assuage his grief and to take his thoughts away from these losses, the old man retired to the pleasant castle of Dornburg on the Saale near Jena, where he finished the *Wanderjahre* in its present form, worked at the Second Part of *Faust*, and revised his scientific writings. In his eighty-first year another great affliction smote him in the death of his only son August, who on account of ill health had gone to Italy, where he died in Rome in 1830. His widow, Ottilie von Goethe, did much to make the last days of the sorrowing father pleasant, and became his favorite. A trip to the Kickelhahn near Ilmenau, where he had spent so many happy days with Karl August, seemed to give him health and vigor. Here, with tears in his eyes, he read the lines which he had written on the wall of a hut many years before:

> "Über allen Gipfeln
> Ist Ruh,
> In allen Wipfeln
> Spürest du
> Kaum einen Hauch;
> Die Vöglein schweigen im Walde.
> Warte nur, balde
> Ruhest du auch."

The expected rest came on the 22d of March, 1832. His last words were, "Licht, mehr Licht!" Thus the grandest poet of German literature passed away and closed the greatest era of poetic achievement in Germany. He was laid to rest in the ducal vault at Weimar near his two friends Schiller and Karl August who had preceded him.

Faust

Faust is Goethe's greatest work and extends over a period of sixty years. The inception reaches back to the epoch of *Götz von Berlichingen*, to a time when the poet regarded all restraints in art and life as troublesome fetters, and justified only the flights of genius; the conclusion of the drama falls in the summer of 1831, only a few months before the poet's death. The work was suggested by the legend of Dr. Faustus, who, as he was represented in the comedies of the sixteenth century, was to the youthful poet the embodiment of the Spirit of the Time, who strove to free himself from every restriction; to the aged poet, however, Faust was the symbol of striving humanity. Goethe's life is so interwoven with the tragedy that it may be considered a commentary on the work. The First Part manifests Goethe's vast knowledge of human thought and affairs, and the final success of an erring seeker after truth.

FIRST PART

This drama is introduced by three prologues. The first is a *Zueignung*, which links the tragedy with the poet's youth; this is followed by the *Vorspiel auf dem Theater*, called by Vischer "a humorous letter of apology," and by the *Prolog im Himmel*, in which the spectator is borne "vom Himmel durch die Welt zur Hölle." The latter is modeled on the opening scene in the Book of Job, and is the key to the drama.

In the first scene we see Faust, an old professor, in a high-vaulted Gothic chamber, weary of study and disgusted with the vanity of knowledge, longing for more freedom and power. He, therefore, turns to magic and summons the spirits to his aid; but when the Earth Spirit says, "Thou'rt like the spirit, thou dost comprehend, not me!" and the spell is interrupted by a visit from Wagner, his "famulus," a "dry-as-dust" pedant, he is very much discouraged, and is about to put a vial of poison to his lips, when he hears the sound of the Easter bells and a chorus chanting "Christ is risen!" This revives a flood of tender recollections of his childhood, and with tears in his eyes he resolves to live.

The next scene is before the city gate on Easter day; students, soldiers, beggars, servant maids, and promenaders of every sort pass out; Faust and Wagner join the motley crowd and walk into the fields, where the "famulus" is greatly impressed with the attention paid the "doctor," but "all this skittle-playing, fiddling, and singing" of the peasants under the linden tree is detestable to him. At sunset they view the landscape, and Faust longs to follow the course of the sun, "his quenchless light to drink, the day before me, and behind the night." A poodle follows them home from the fields and reveals himself as Mephistopheles,—the Spirit who evermore denies,—in the guise of a traveling scholar. After Mephistopheles has offered Faust his services he calls his spirits to lull Faust to sleep.

We now come to the magnificent scene in which Faust signs the compact with his own blood; Mephistopheles says:

> "I'll pledge myself to be thy servant *here*,
> Still at thy back alert and prompt to be;
> But when together *yonder* we appear,
> Then shalt thou do the same for me."

Faust agrees to this on the condition that Mephistopheles shall so satisfy his soul with the pleasures of life that he can say to the passing moment, "Linger awhile, so fair thou art." While Faust is preparing for his new life, Mephistopheles, disguised as a professor, gives some evil advice to a student, who listens submissively and then begs him to write a few lines in his album as a token of his favor. Mephistopheles writes these words: "Eritis sicut Deus, scientes bonum et malum," and the guileless student departs well satisfied.

Faust is now introduced to a number of jovial students who are drinking, singing, and quarreling in Auerbach's wine cellar in Leipzig, but he is disgusted with the scene. He is not yet prepared to enjoy such buffoonery, and Mephistopheles takes him to the Witches' Kitchen. Here he drinks a magic potion to restore his youthful vigor, and sees in a mirror the form of a beautiful maiden. Now the old, gray-haired professor is changed into a handsome and passionate youth, and the Gretchen tragedy begins.

Margaret first appears on the scene as she comes from the church and repulses Faust when he seeks to escort her home. Not discouraged at this, Faust and his companion succeed in placing a casket of jewels in Margaret's room. When Faust learns that Margaret's mother has given the gems to a priest, he begs Mephistopheles to "bring fresh jewels instantly." These she does not show to her mother, but carries them to Martha, a wicked neighbor, who with Mephistopheles arranges a meeting with Faust and Margaret in her garden. Here Margaret innocently tells Faust the story of her life, and they soon fall in love, while Martha entertains Mephistopheles with a marriage proposition. Enticed thus by the devil, Faust and Margaret succumb to his wiles. Withdrawing to a cavern in the forest, Faust spends his time in contemplation, until Mephistopheles comes and chides him for neglecting Margaret, who is continually longing for him. Meanwhile Margaret spends her time in loneliness and spins as she sings:

> "My heart is heavy, my peace is o'er;
> I shall find it never; oh, never more!"

The lovers meet again in the garden and Margaret, with childlike simplicity, is now made the unconscious instrument of her mother's death. Margaret then questions Faust about his religion. Subsequent scenes represent Margaret at the well, and before the Mater Dolorosa, where her own sins appear to her blacker than before, and she prays to be delivered from disgrace and death. Valentine, her soldier-brother, hears of her shame and returns home only to fall at the hands of Margaret's betrayer. There is now no peace for the poor girl, for even in the Cathedral she is pursued by the Evil Spirit, and the deep tones of the organ and the words of the chorus seem to condemn her. Soon afterwards she is arrested and imprisoned for infanticide. While she is pining in the dungeon, Mephistopheles makes a final attempt to distract Faust by leading him to the Brocken on "Walpurgisnacht," but not even the brilliant and exciting scenes of the witches' carnival can make him forget Margaret. Driven almost to madness Faust commands Mephistopheles to save her. The final scene of the tragedy pictures Margaret and Faust in the dungeon to which Faust has come before daybreak to save her from the hands of the executioner, but her mind has been so affected by the terrible strain that she does not recognize her lover, and thinking it is the headsman she hides her head in a bed of straw. But when he calls her by name she knows his voice and embraces and caresses him. While she recalls her past and expresses a wish concerning the final disposition of her body, Faust continues to urge her to flee with him; but at the appearance of Mephistopheles, she shrinks back in horror and can not be persuaded to leave the prison. Mephistopheles sees that he has failed in his purpose, and scornfully cries out, "She is judged!" but voices from above reply, "She is saved!" As Faust is hurried away by his companion, Margaret's pleading voice is heard faintly calling, "Henry! Henry!"

SECOND PART

The Second Part represents Faust's experiences in the "Greater World," which encompasses all the influences and activities of man, and offers an opportunity to atone for sin by useful service. It is often obscure and unintelligible, and admits only of symbolic interpretation, but the true spirit of altruism is clearly discernible throughout. We must suppose that considerable time has elapsed between the two parts of the tragedy. The scenes up to the fourth act "shift from land to land, as in a phantasmagoria."

The first scene pictures Faust reclining upon a flowery turf, seeking sleep, and surrounded by a circle of spirits. When he awakens a beautiful sunrise in the Alps greets him, and having forgotten the past, and feeling refreshed, he starts out with Mephistopheles to make himself useful in the world. They first appear at the court of an emperor, whom they help out of financial troubles. Here Faust gives an exhibition of his art, and summons the shades of Paris and Helen from Hades. Helen is so beautiful that Faust falls in love with her and desires to possess her, but as he attempts to embrace her she vanishes.

In the second act Faust and Wagner are together in the study as of old; Faust sleeps, while Wagner is creating a homunculus. To cure Faust of his passion for Helen, Mephistopheles and Homunculus carry him away to the classical Walpurgis Night. Not finding her here he descends into Hades in search of her.

The third act opens with Helen's return from Troy. She fears that Menelaus, believing her guilty of infidelity, is planning to sacrifice her to the gods. Mephistopheles offers to deliver her, and she is transported to Faust's Arcadian castle, where they are married. A son, Euphorion, is born to them, who, defying all restraints, attempts to fly, and "falls dead at the feet of his parents." His spirit vanishes and draws his mother after him. Faust tries to hold her, but only her garments remain, and these soon turn into clouds and bear him away.

In the next act we find Faust on a mountain top in Germany. Mephistopheles begins to realize that Faust is growing away from him, and tries to lure him with promises of earthly power and political aggrandizement. Thinking that political life will afford him an opportunity for doing good, Faust aids in quelling a rebellion against the emperor. As a reward the emperor gives him a large tract of marshy land which he drains and prepares for human habitation and industries.

In the last act Faust is a hundred years old, physically strong, and active in intellect, but still unsatisfied; the moment has not yet come to which he can say, "Linger awhile, so fair thou art!"

Wherever he seeks to do good, Mephistopheles and his spirits mingle evil with it. After the burning of the cottage of the two peasants, Faust is visited at his castle by four gray women,—Want, Guilt, Care, and Need; Faust closes his door, and only Care steals in through the keyhole, but although she strikes him with blindness, she can not overcome him. Death now appears, but Faust does not see him; he still strives on unselfishly to provide homes for men. As he comes forth from his palace groping his way, the clang of spades delights his soul; he thinks his vassals are carrying on his work, but they are the Lemures digging his grave. Having now accomplished his purpose and reached the moment of highest enjoyment, Faust sinks upon the soil which he has reclaimed, and dies with the anticipation of future happiness. Mephistopheles and his hosts now contend with the angels for the soul of Faust and are defeated; strewing roses, and rising higher as they bear the immortal part of Faust away, the angels sing:

> "Saved is this noble soul from ill,
>   Our spirit peer. Whoever
> Strives forward with unswerving will,—
>   Him can we aye deliver."

THE PERIOD OF TRANSITION

THE German Empire suffered greatly at the beginning of the nineteenth century by the victorious invasion of Napoleon, against whom no united and powerful resistance was made. But when the French became more and more the oppressors of the Germans, the princes as well as their subjects united to overthrow their powerful enemy. More than fifty years were necessary to restore a proper adjustment of the political affairs of the different states. German literature in the first half of the century bears no individual stamp. In part it reflects the movement called forth by the political struggles, but for the most part it reverted from subjects of public interest and followed the classical movement inaugurated by Schiller and Goethe, or else was limited to provincial and dialectic poetry.

In the transition from the classicism of the eighteenth century to the romanticism of the nineteenth we find a truly great writer in JEAN PAUL RICHTER (1763–1825). In him we find the harmonious individual so earnestly sought in classic German literature. With the two dramatists Iffland and Kotzebue, the former of whom stood in close relation to Schiller, while the latter made himself a reputation as the enemy of Goethe, stands Jean Paul, who helped make Weimar famous. He is characterized by a strong imagination, incoherent sentences, sudden changes from jest to earnest, and the numerous long ramifications in his narratives. His humor and sentimentality enabled him to picture landscapes in the most fantastic colors, and to criticise severely the society of his day and the weakness of the smaller German states. The most important of his romances are *Titan* and *Flegeljahre*. Among his purely humorous writings, *Dr. Katzenbergers Badereise* is perhaps the best. Because of his eccentric and intricate style and language his works are seldom translated or read.

ROMANTICISM

At the close of the eighteenth century all branches of culture received attention. The classical spirit had been reinstated in German literature; but the forces which had been active in the "Sturm und Drang" again manifested themselves, and produced a revolt against classicism, known as Romanticism. The writers of the EARLY ROMANTIC SCHOOL were subjective, bound by no rules, and allowed the imagination full sway. Their aim was to revive mediaeval chivalry and romance, to reproduce fantastic myths, and to animate anew the patriotic feeling of the nation. The movement influenced all the sciences, religion, and poetry, and made prominent such men as SCHLEIERMACHER and the brothers JACOB and

WILHELM GRIMM. The former is known by his religious writings, and the Grimms by their *Kinder- und Hausmärchen,* and their unfinished German dictionary.

The real soul of the new tendency was FRIEDRICH SCHLEGEL (1772–1829), who, after teaching at various universities, finally settled in Vienna as a member of the Austrian chancery. He is notable for his studies in philosophy and aesthetics, for his histories of ancient and modern literature, and for bringing the ideas of romanticism into a more intellectual form. His most valuable work is a treatise, *Über die Sprache und Weisheit der Indier.* His brother, AUGUST WILHELM SCHLEGEL (1767–1845), gave free vent to his inclinations. He served as professor at Jena a few years, then accompanied Madame de Staël to Italy, Denmark, and Sweden, and finally became a professor at the University of Bonn. He won his reputation by his translations from Dante, Calderon, and Shakespeare, and was of greater literary importance than his brother.

LUDWIG TIECK (1773–1853) was very popular at the beginning of the century as the author of several dramas in which he developed all the ideas of the Romantic School. Among his early stories we may mention *William Lovell.* His most important works are *Kaiser Octavianus* and *Genoveva.* Among the best of his fairy tales published in his book *Phantasus* are *Der getreue Eckart, Die Elven, Der Blaubart,* and

Rotkäppchen. While Tieck manifests great skill in depicting scenery, he nevertheless lacks depth and emotion. Contemporaneously with his *Märchen* appeared several satirical comedies like *Der gestiefelte Kater*, perhaps the best drama of this class in German literature, and the romance *Franz Sternbalds Wanderungen*, written in conjunction with W. H. Wackenroder. In 1819 Tieck was dramaturgist in Dresden, and later was called to Berlin by Frederick William IV., where he remained until his death. In this epoch of his life he wrote most of his novels. Together with A. W. Schlegel he was to translate Shakespeare, but he left his share of the work to be done by others, chiefly by his daughter. His ability as a translator is seen in his translation of Cervantes' romance *Don Quixote.* His poems are of little importance.

FRIEDRICH VON HARDENBERG, called NOVALIS (1772–1801), is as a poet more important than Tieck. His *Hymnen an die Nacht*, written in memory of his betrothed, reveal a tenderness and depth of feeling not to be found in Tieck. His life was short and therefore many of his other works were left unfinished. His *Geistliche Lieder* are good and are sung even to this day, but of the seven romances which he had planned to write, only the first part of one, *Heinrich von Ofterdingen*, modeled on *Wilhelm Meister*, was completed. He is considered the most talented poet of the Early Romantic School.

Through the influence of Tieck and the Schlegel brothers a number of young men became interested in literary work and formed the Later School of Romanticism. They differed from the poets of the Early School in paying less attention to their theoretical views, and more to real work, and therefore were able to produce works of greater importance; but they imitated them in their fantastic ideas and choice of strange subjects.

E. T. A. HOFFMANN (1776–1822), one of the most gifted of the later Romanticists, exerted a wide and lasting influence. His artistic style and wonderful imaginative power enabled him to portray supernatural horrors in a remarkably realistic manner. Characteristic among his works are *Nachtstücke, Die Serapionsbrüder*, and the fantastic romance *Lebens-Ansichten des Katers Murr*.

CLEMENS BRENTANO (1778–1842), wrote lyrics and novels, among which are *Godwi, oder das steinerne Bild der Mutter*, the charming *Geschichte vom braven Kasperl und der schönen Annerl*, and *Das Märchen von Gockel, Hinkel und Gackeleia*. *Des Knaben Wunderhorn* (1805–08), a collection of German *Volkslieder*, was published conjointly with LUDWIG ACHIM VON ARNIM (1781–1831). The latter married Bettina, Brentano's sister, whose charming productions prove that she, too, was a writer of no little ability.

Another follower of the Schlegels was FRIEDRICH

Baron de la Motte Fouqué (1777–1843). Although of an ancient French family he served in the German army and then devoted himself to literature. His best work is *Undine*, a charming story of a water sprite who lives with a fisherman and his wife, and then becomes the bride of a knight, and is endowed with a soul. When called upon to suffer human disappointment and sorrow she returns to her native element. The principal representatives of the drama of this romantic period are F. L. Zacharias Werner and Heinrich von Kleist; the former is almost forgotten to-day, but his fate tragedy, *Der vierundzwanzigste Februar*, introduced a series of "Schicksalstragödien," in imitation of Schiller's *Die Braut von Messina*.

Heinrich von Kleist (1777–1811), one of the most original dramatists of North Germany, was inspired by the patriotic enthusiasm which brought forth the War of Liberation. He was of a morbid and fanciful disposition, but some of his works are remarkable for poetic feeling and real dramatic ability. Doomed to repeated disappointment, unhappy in love, discouraged by Goethe's harsh criticism, he committed suicide when he was only thirty-four years of age. In his tragedy *Die Familie Schroffenstein* he shows how two noble families, blinded by hatred and suspicion, can ruin each other. *Das Kätchen von Heilbronn*, his most popular drama, presents a heroine whose character is possible only by the intervention of supernatural power. *Der zerbrochene Krug* is a bright little comedy giving a scene in a village court, in which the judge himself is discovered to be the culprit. Of Kleist's eight novels, *Michael Kohlhaas* is the best. Dreams and somnambulism play an important part in the drama *Prinz Friedrich von Homburg*. The last of his dramas, *Die Hermanns-schlacht*, treats of the Cheruscan prince Arminius, who drove the Romans out of Germany. This hero is held up to the petty German princes of Kleist's own time as a model in their efforts to throw off the French yoke.

Chamisso, Eichendorff, and Müller, who resembled the Romanticists in general mode of thought, but excelled in the freshness of their style of presentation, belong to the most popular poets of the nineteenth century.

ADELBERT VON CHAMISSO (1781–1838), was a Frenchman by birth, who, when nine years of age, fled with his parents to Berlin, and later entered the German army. He was preëminently a lyric poet and knew well how to give expression to his moods and feelings. *Das Schloss Boncourt* expresses a lament for the home of his childhood, while the cycles of poems *Frauen-Liebe und Leben* and *Lebenslieder und Bilder* tell of the experiences of everyday life. Best of all is the poem *Salas y Gomez*, which describes the life of a shipwrecked man on a desert island in the ocean; in it we see the influences of the poet's trip around the world. His story of *Peter Schlemihl*, the man who sold his shadow for an inexhaustible sum of money, and his excellent description of his travels rank him as a prose writer of considerable ability.

The last distinguished Romanticist, JOSEPH FREI-HERR VON EICHENDORFF (1788–1857), studied in Breslau, Halle, and also in Heidelberg, where he came into touch with Brentano and Arnim, whom he assisted in the publication of the *Wunderhorn*. Inspired by his rare spirituality and love of home and nature, he was without doubt the greatest lyric poet of the Romantic Movement. His *Wanderlieder* reveal that national inclination to travel so characteristic of many of the earlier German poets, and are among the best of his collection of *Gedichte*. As a prose writer, Eichendorff is known only through his masterpiece, *Aus dem Leben eines Taugenichts*. This story is full of good humor and tells of a dreamy, buoyant young musician who starts out to see the world and falls in love with a supposed young countess; thinking that she is already betrothed he again wanders out into the world, and when he returns he finds she is still true to her " Taugenichts."

Another master of the popular lyric is the North German WILHELM MÜLLER (1794–1827), father of the celebrated philologist Max Müller. He wrote a few ballads and a few excellent drinking and love songs; of the former only *Der Glockenguss zu Breslau* has become popular. Among the latter are some of the choicest lyrics of the time, as *Der Lindenbaum, Jägers Lust, Das Wandern ist des Müllers Lust,* and his drinking song *Im Krug zum grünen Kranze.* The *Lieder der Griechen,* published near the close of his short and wayward life, are full of sentimental patriotism.

HEINRICH ZSCHOKKE (1771–1848), was born in Magdeburg, and lived in Switzerland from the time he was twenty-five years of age. Besides *Stunden der Andacht,* which has become a household book in Switzerland, he wrote many stories, noteworthy among them being *Das Goldmacherdorf,* on the model of Pestalozzi's *Lienhard und Gertrud,* and the series of novels *Bilder aus der Schweiz.*

Chief among the historical novelists who wrote under the influence of Scott, was the North German WILHELM HÄRING (1798–1871), better known by the pseudonym WILLIBALD ALEXIS, whose novels served to inspire patriotic feeling in Germany at a time of political unrest and national depression. Alexis was also a journalist of considerable reputation, but his fame now rests upon his series of historical novels, of which the best are *Der Roland von Berlin, Der falsche Waldemar, Die Hosen des Herrn von Bredow,* and *Ruhe ist die erste Bürgerpflicht.*

Hölderlin, Platen, and Rückert,—although in some respects resembling the Romanticists,—are masters of form, and show great skill in the use of the most difficult meters.

FRIEDRICH HÖLDERLIN (1770–1843), stood in closest relation to the Romanticists in that he sought to adjust the ideal to the real. He was a lover of classical antiquity, and wrote a romance, *Hyperion*, in which he describes in beautiful language the hopes and the disappointments of a young Greek who takes part in the struggle of his people against the Turks; but it is as a lyric poet that we see him to the best advantage. He was greatly influenced by Schiller in his earliest writings.

KARL GEORG AUGUST, GRAF VON PLATEN-HALLERMÜNDE (1796–1835), was an aristocrat, and too self-confident and unpatriotic to win the sympathy of his people. Most of his life was spent in Italy and Greece. He was noted as a linguist, and his lyrical poems include several odes, hymns, and sonnets, which are among the best in the German language. Among his best ballads we find *Das Grab im Busento* and *Der Pilgrim von St. Just*. Platen makes use of fairy tales in his comedy *Der gläserne Pantoffel*, and in his epic *Die Abbassiden*, which relates the adventures of the sons of Harun-al-Raschid after the manner of Wieland's *Oberon*. In *Die verhängnissvolle Gabel*, Platen satirizes the "Schicksalstragödie," while *Der romantische Ödipus* is directed more against the plays of Immermann, and Romanticism in general.

FRIEDRICH RÜCKERT (1788–1866), ranks next to Platen in the mastery of language and verse, but he

lacked self-concentration and dramatic ability.   He
was in his early years a singer of the War of Liberation, and wrote *Kriegerische Spott- und Ehrenlieder*,
and other war songs which greatly stirred the hearts
of the German people.   Some of his political poems,
such as *Barbarossa*, *Die drei Gesellen*, and *Die Gräber
zu Ottensen* are still national favorites.   Later in life
he turned his attention to the study of the people and
the literature of the Orient, which is best illustrated
by his collection of poems *Östliche Rosen*, and by
a version of the Persian *Rostem und Suhrab*.   Rückert describes his own love and courtship in *Liebes-
frühling*,—a collection of about 350 poems,—and presents his own ideas of philosophy in *Die Weisheit des
Brahmanen*, a collection of poems in six volumes.

The Poets of the War of Liberation

The War of Liberation (1813–1815) marks a brief
period in the history of German literature.   The desire for liberty was awakened in the hearts of all the
people and intense hatred of the French was everywhere manifest.   Among the younger poets not one
could be found who would not willingly have used
his poetical ability in the service of the Fatherland;
Fouqué, Schulze, Eichendorff, Müller, Rückert,
Uhland, and many others contributed to stir the fire
of patriotism.   Arndt, Körner, and Schenkendorf
animated and encouraged the people most by their
patriotic and glowing war songs.

ERNST MORITZ ARNDT (1769–1860) wrote the best patriotic lyrics of this period. His poetry was inspired by the spirit of the Volkslied and the spiritual fervor which characterized the German revolt against Napoleon. Like Luther, he seemed like a religious reformer who knew how to arouse, animate, and foster a conviction of true patriotism and sincerity. With enthusiasm the Germans sang *Der Gott, der Eisen wachsen liess*, *Was ist des Deutschen Vaterland?* and *Deutsches Herz, verzage nicht*. His balladlike songs such as *Das Lied vom Schill* and *Die Leipziger Schlacht*, as also his religious hymns, were scarcely less popular.

KARL THEODOR KÖRNER (1791–1813) became a favorite with the German people more through his personality and his fate than through the merit of his productions. He learned much from his association with Schiller, whom his father had befriended in Leipzig and Dresden. When Frederick William III called for troops, Körner's youthful patriotism was aroused and he joined Lützow's cavalry as a volunteer. During the five months of his service he wrote those charming songs which were later collected under the title *Leier und Schwert*. His most popular songs are *Gebet während der Schlacht*, *Lützows wilde Jagd*, and the *Schwertlied*, written just before his death. His dramas, which were written within one year, show a lack of maturity in experience and knowledge. His best drama is *Zriny*, which is taken from

Hungarian history, and has been played not only in Austria and Germany, but also in America.

MAXIMILIAN VON SCHENKENDORF (1783–1817) resembled the Romanticists in his fondness for the splendor of the Middle Ages. His lyrics are characterized by religious zeal and enthusiasm for the hoped-for revival of the empire. Although less aggressive than either Körner or Arndt, he nevertheless was more thoughtful, and produced lyrics of a higher value. His patriotism is manifested in such songs as *Landsturm*, *Das Lied vom Rhein*, and in the poems *Freiheit* and *Muttersprache*. Some of his patriotic songs were composed for special occasions, as *Soldaten-Morgenlied*, *Auf Scharnhorsts Tod*, and the ballad *Andreas Hofer*. His poems are full of sympathy and feeling and express the hope that the empire may be united and strong.

THE SWABIAN SCHOOL; AUSTRIAN WRITERS

The Swabian poets "carried the Romantic traditions across the uninspired period of political journalism, which arose under 'Young Germany,' and kept the line unbroken between the leaders of Romanticism and masters like Storm and Keller in the following generation." But while the Romanticists sought their material in the fables of the Orient, or in the romances of the Middle Ages, these poets turned their attention to the rivers, woods, and mountains around them, and drew their inspiration from their own beloved "Schwabenland." The leader of this circle was LUDWIG UHLAND (1787–1862), who early showed great talent, and was destined for the legal profession, but later became professor in the University of Tübingen. His life was an intermixture of political struggles, poetic activity, and educational service. He represents all that was best in later Romanticism, and found much to admire in the history of his own people. He revised, enlarged, and systematically arranged the collection of folk songs which had been begun by Herder and continued by Arnim and Brentano. Uhland's poetry has the merit of genuineness and bears the stamp of his own individuality. He excels as a writer of lyric-epics. His poems may conveniently be divided into four classes:

1. Poems which have no definite historical or geographical background, such as *Das Schloss am Meer*, *Des Sängers Fluch*, *Der Wirtin Töchterlein*, and *Der gute Kamerad*.

2. Poems which are based on Northern or Swabian sagas and history, as *Der blinde König*, *Siegfried und Rolandlieder*, *Tells Tod* and *Schwäbische Kunde*.

3. Poems whose material was taken from French and English history, as *Bertran de Born*, *Taillefer*, *Harald*, and *Das Glück von Edenhall*.

4. Poems which refer to scenes in Spain, as *Die Bidassoabrücke* and *Der Waller*.

To these may be added a few allegorical poems,

and some lyrics, which appear as patriotic, hunting, and drinking songs, as *Jägerlied, Einkehr,* and *Die Kapelle.* Uhland's dramas show little dramatic talent, and only limited knowledge of theatrical requirements, as may be seen in the two historical dramas *Ernst, Herzog von Schwaben,* and *Ludwig der Bayer.*

With Uhland we must mention JUSTINUS A. C. KERNER and GUSTAV SCHWAB; the former, a physician in Weinsberg, wrote on visionary subjects, and leads the reader into the region of dreams and mysteries, as in *Die Seherin von Prevorst;*—the latter, a clergyman, possessed a cheerful disposition, and wrote on a variety of subjects, but as a poet he was inferior to both Uhland and Kerner. He is perhaps best remembered by his student song *Bemooster Bursche zieh' ich aus.*

Among the Swabian writers not directly connected with the "Dichterbund" are EDUARD MÖRIKE, who wrote beautiful lyrics, novels, and the interesting story *Mozart auf der Reise nach Prag,* and WILHELM HAUFF, remembered as the author of the historical romance *Lichtenstein,*—in close imitation of Scott,—and *Phantasien im Bremer Rathskeller.* As a poet he is best known by his *Reiters Morgengesang* and *Soldatenliebe.*

ANASTASIUS GRÜN (Anton Alexander Graf von Auersperg), made himself popular throughout Germany by his liberal political views. His romance

Der letzte Ritter glorifies Maximilian I and imitates
Uhland in kindly humor and earnestness. JOSEPH
CHRISTIAN FREIHERR VON ZEDLITZ followed the tra-
ditions of the Romantic school. Among his best
ballads are *Nächtliche Heerschau, Das Geisterschiff,
Das Weib des Räubers*, and *Mariechen.* His best
work is *Todtenkränze.* Among the Austrian writers
LENAU is the most important lyric poet, and GRILL-
PARZER the best dramatist.

Deep melancholy hangs like a cloud over all the
writings of NIKOLAUS LENAU (1802–50), who has
been called "Der Dichter des Schmerzes." Neither
in Austria nor in America could he find freedom from
religious doubt and pessimism. Nature had a peculiar fascination for him, as is shown in his exquisite
and touching *Schilflieder* and *Haidebilder;* and what
could be more pathetic than his *Bitte an die Nacht.*
His poems *Niagara, Das Blockhaus*, and *Der In-
dianerzug* illustrate his pessimistic impressions of
America. In his longer works, *Faust, Savonarola*,
and *Die Albigenser*, he manifests a despair which is
characteristic of the literature of his country even
to this day. Stricken with paralysis, and partially
insane, he was taken to Austria, where he died in
1850.

FRANZ GRILLPARZER (1791–1872), was the foremost of the Austrian poets who were influenced by
the Romantic movement, but only late in life was he
permitted to enjoy the favor and recognition which

he merited. Grillparzer was passionate and quick-tempered, and a pietistic vein runs through all his plays. As a dramatist he surpassed all his contemporaries, taking his models from the classics and the Spanish writers. His dramas are characterized by fullness of thought, a rapid succession of events, and true dramatic life. His fate tragedy, *Die Ahnfrau*, in which the ancestress appears when any evil is about to happen to the ill-fated family, and *Sappho*, whose unhappy love and tragic death are told in beautiful verse, made the poet famous. The latter, as also the trilogy *Das goldene Vliess*,—the symbol of destruction and man's guilt,—and *Des Meeres und der Liebe Wellen* (Hero and Leander), treat in a masterly manner material taken from Greek literature. His historical dramas *König Ottokars Glück und Ende, Ein treuer Diener seines Herrn*, and *Ein Bruderzwist im Hause Habsburg* were greatly influenced by Schiller. In his tragedy *Die Jüdin von Toledo*, Lope de Vega's influence is seen, while in his masterpiece, *Der Traum ein Leben*, both French and Spanish material was used. The last complete work which he was permitted to see presented on the stage, the comedy *Weh' dem, der lügt*, was so poorly received that the poet felt offended, and made no further attempts to please the public. Although his countrymen were slow to recognize his rare gifts, he was accorded at the close of his life a part of that favor and appreciation which were due him. He lies buried near Beethoven, who, with Haydn and Mozart, was among his favorite musicians.

"YOUNG GERMANY"

After the War of Liberation was over, a group of writers, vaguely called "Das junge Deutschland," attempted to revolutionize German literature. In respect to social, political, and religious institutions, their tendencies were generally negative; they repudiated the spirit of Romanticism, but they had nothing better to offer, and used literature merely to further their political ambitions, and to give expression to their personal views on the social questions of the time; the Bundesrat, however, forbade the publication of these writings in 1835. Although, as literary reformers, the "Young German" writers were a failure, they no doubt assisted in advancing the interests of society, church, and literature, by imitating French models. Two main classes manifested themselves,—the one advocated the complete overthrow of existing conditions, the other delighted in the description of the wanton and tragic scenes of life. To the latter class belong the "unruly genius" CHRISTIAN DIETRICH GRABBE (1801–36), whose plays are marred by the absurd declamation with which they abound; OTTO LUDWIG (1813–65), who gained a reputation through the tragedies *Der Erbförster* and *Die Makkabäer*, and the excellent novel *Zwischen Himmel und Erde;* and CHRISTIAN

FRIEDRICH HEBBEL (1813–63), the son of a poor mason in Holstein, who by persistent efforts acquired an education, and rose to be a dramatist of note. He was original and thorough, and exerted a powerful influence on the development of the German drama. His first tragedy, *Judith*, is characterized by strong passions and horrible incidents, but it was played in Berlin and made the author celebrated. *Maria Magdalena*, a burgher tragedy, represents the tragic conflict resulting from the modern man's inability to adjust himself properly to his environment. Other dramas completed at this time are *Genoveva*, *Herodes und Mariamne*, and *Agnes Bernauer*. In his masterpiece, *Gyges und sein Ring*, Hebbel combined the tragic themes of all his former works, and shows a tendency toward realism. His trilogy *Die Nibelungen* resembles Wagner's opera of the same name in the legendary-epic material treated, and also in its artistic purposes. *Demetrius*, his last drama, like Schiller's, remained unfinished.

Among the well-known revolutionary writers is LUDWIG BÖRNE, a converted Jew, who devoted himself to journalism, and became one of the most bitter adversaries of the government. In his *Briefe aus Paris* he shows himself to be a masterly political pamphleteer. Other leaders of this movement were HEINRICH LAUBE and KARL F. GUTZKOW. Laube was also a journalist, and was greatly influenced by Schiller. One of his best romances is *Das junge*

Europa, in which the author discusses the advanced
ideas of his time. Gutzkow, whom we may consider
a real leader of "Young Germany," was a journalist
of considerable note, and displayed much ability as a
novelist and dramatist, but his productions were
often marred by his bitter criticism and harsh judgment of the existing moral and social conditions.
His romance *Die Ritter vom Geiste,* in nine volumes,
is a description of the evils of modern society, with a
possible remedy, and may be considered a forerunner
of the modern social novel in Germany. Among
his remaining novels are *Der Zauberer von Rom* and
Hohenschwangau. In his most successful drama,
Uriel Acosta, he favors freedom of opinion, and presents tragic situations in a forcible manner. Among
his best works is the historical comedy *Zopf und
Schwert,* which reflects the time of Friedrich Wilhelm I of Prussia. Prominent among the lyric writers of this movement are GEORG HERWEGH, known
by such poems as *Reiterlied* and *Strophen aus der
Fremde;* HERMANN FERDINAND FREILIGRATH, by
his volume of political poems *Ein Glaubensbekennt-
niss,* and other poems like *O lieb' so lang' du lieben
kannst;* and HOFFMANN VON FALLERSLEBEN, as a
writer of excellent Volkslieder, of which *Deutschland,
Deutschland über alles* has attained well-deserved
popularity. "Young Germany" met opposition in
writers like KARL L. IMMERMANN, who satirizes the
spirit of the time in his best romance, *Münchhausen,*

and truthfully portrays society, showing the bright as well as the dark side of life, and in patriots like EMAN-UEL GEIBEL, who did not approve of the introduction of French influence and models in German literature. Possessed of deep piety, and free from bitter party feeling, Geibel longed to see Germany united. In his collections of political poems he manifests a conciliatory spirit, but little individuality. Other poems have become popular through the love of freedom and the Christian principles which they express.

In direct contrast with Geibel's serious contemplative nature stands HEINRICH HEINE (1799–1856), the most talented of all the writers who were associated with "Young Germany." The son of Jewish parents, he was destined for a commercial career; but this was distasteful to him and he took up the study of law at Bonn and Göttingen, and then went to Berlin, where he was welcomed to a literary circle which met at the home of Varnhagen von Ense. Here he published his first collection of poems, followed in 1823 by two tragedies, *Almansor* and *William Ratcliff*, which attracted little attention. After a short stay at Cuxhaven he returned to Göttingen and received his degree in 1825. While here he made a tour of the Harz Mountains, an account of which is given in his *Harzreise*, which brought him renown. In these years he planned a *Faust*, and wrote the novel-fragment *Der Rabbi von Bacharach*. Before he left Göttingen and took up the legal profession, he embraced the Christian faith. During the next five years he published his *Reisebilder* and *Buch der Lieder*, upon which his popularity rests. With the simple language of the folk song, the graphic descriptions of Goethe, and the emotional ballad style of Bürger, he wrote some of the most charming love songs and romances to be found in the German language. Who has not been touched by the beauty and pathos in *Die Wallfahrt nach Kevlaar* and *An meine Mutter*? But he lacked moral balance, and indulged in much bitter satire, attacking friend and enemy alike; his attacks on the government became so hostile that he was declared an outlaw. In 1831 he went to Paris, where he spent the remainder of his life. Here as journalist and literary critic he manifested his contempt for Germany and German literature. In 1843 his *Atta Troll, ein Sommernachtstraum*, was written, and was followed the next year by *Deutschland, ein Wintermärchen*. Confined to his bed by a spinal disease from 1848 until his death in 1856, he composed his *Romanzero*, in some respects his noblest work. No other German poet has so charmingly described the sea, which to Heine symbolized "the seething unrest of human life"; no lyric poet has been more widely read, nor has exerted a more lasting influence. "Heine," says Matthew Arnold, "is incomparably the most important figure of that quarter of a century that follows the death of Goethe."

THE MODERN PERIOD

THE exclusion of Austria from the confederacy of German states in 1866, and the transference of the hereditary imperial authority to the ruling house of Prussia in 1871, solved the political problem for Imperial Germany. A new era for the development of the political, social, and economic conditions of Germany had come. The influence which the new ideas exerted on the literature of this period has manifested itself in the national consciousness of the German people and in the realism so character-istic of modern literature. On the threshold of this period stands RICHARD WAGNER (1813–83), a writer and composer by whom the national character was stimulated in the modern musical drama. His pro-ductions mark the beginning of a new epoch in the development of the German theater. He found the material for his dramas in the national sagas, and knew how to give the proper poetic, musical, and scenic expression to them. As early as 1842 Wagner's *Rienzi* demonstrated his remarkable artistic ability as a dramatic composer. While in Paris the next year Wagner composed *Der fliegende Holländer*, which was followed by *Tannhäuser* in 1845, and *Lohengrin* in 1850. His next work, *Der Ring des Nibelungen*,

1853, is a trilogy; the first drama, *Die Walküre*, is preceded by a "Vorabend," *Das Rheingold;* the second drama is called *Siegfried*, and the third, *Götterdämmerung*. Two other masterpieces, *Tristan und Isolde*, 1865, and the comedy *Die Meistersinger von Nürnberg*, 1868, added to the composer's well-earned fame. His last work, *Parsifal*, 1882, was not received with as much enthusiasm by the younger generation as was accorded some of his earlier dramas. Wagner's operas are presented every summer in the theater he himself built at Bayreuth, in Bavaria.

The literature of this period, in addition to Wagner's music dramas, is represented by a long list of able writers, who, in the novel and drama, show great individuality and a strong democratic spirit. The influence of TOLSTOY and IBSEN is manifest in no small degree in the later writings of this age.

Among the novelists who were active in the preceding as well as in the modern period is GUSTAV FREYTAG (1816–95). As a dramatist he evinced much talent early in his literary career, and although some of his dramas are now considered of mediocre grade, his comedy *Die Journalisten* (1852) is still popular. His *Technik des Dramas*, written ten years later, is a valuable treatise on dramaturgy. *Soll und Haben* (1855), written in praise of German commercialism, and translated into different languages, is perhaps his best novel. *Die verlorene Handschrift* (1864) is more artificial than the preceding novel and treats of scholarly society. In his *Bilder aus der deutschen Vergangenheit* (1859–62), he gives the German people a well-written history of their past which he supplements with a group of romances, called *Die Ahnen* (1872–80).

Another novelist who treats of the social tendencies of his time is FRIEDRICH SPIELHAGEN (b. 1829), who became known through his *Problematische Naturen* (1860), which is completed in *Durch Nacht zum Licht*, and shows that in all human endeavors there is a unity and solidarity of interests. The same ideas prevail in *Die von Hohenstein* (1864), *In Reih und Glied* (1866), and *Hammer und Amboss* (1869). In 1876 appeared *Sturmflut*, which compares the struggles in society and the financial world after the Franco-German War, with a storm on the shores of the Baltic Sea, and may be considered one of his best works. Although he was always in sympathy with the literary movements of the day, many of his recent novels have not become very popular.

The provincial novel, which had been cultivated by JOHANN PETER HEBEL of Basel, who pictured scenes in the Black Forest, in the dialect of the people, was revived a generation later by BERTHOLD AUERBACH (1812–82). He was a man of Jewish extraction, and being a native of the Black Forest he naturally portrayed in his novels the life and customs of this locality. His first novel, *Spinoza*, was followed in

1843 by a collection of stories under the title *Schwarz-wälder Dorfgeschichten*, which immediately attracted attention. The spirit, beauty, and charm of the Swabian dialect are found in all these tales. In his well-known novels *Die Frau Professorin* (1846) and *Barfüssele* (1857) he shows a tendency to philoso-phize, while in the long novels *Auf der Höhe* and *Das Landhaus am Rhein* he attempts to apply his Spinozan philosophy to the social problems of his age. *Waldfried* (1874) has a political background. Later in life Auerbach returned to the "Village Tale" and wrote *Nach dreissig Jahren, Der Forst-meister*, and *Brigitta*. Another writer of provincial novels is FRITZ REUTER (1810–74), a North German humorist who wrote in the "Plattdeutsch" dialect. While a student he was arrested for wearing the colors of a political club, and was condemned to death, but the sentence was commuted to thirty years' imprisonment. After serving a part of his sentence he was released and wrote *Läuschen und Riemels*, a collection of short stories and rhymes. His next work *Ut de Franzosentid* was followed by *Ut mine Festungstid* and *Ut mine Stromtid*, which are autobiographical in character. Besides KARL VON HOLTEI, who wrote poems in the Silesian dialect, we must here mention the democratic Austrian, LUDWIG ANZENGRUBER (1839–89), who has written his chief works in dialect, and stands for all that is best in the provincial novel. A wholesome optimism

pervades his works; and, more of a realist than
Auerbach, he does not idealize his peasants but
pictures them as they really are. Two of his best
dramas, *Die Kreuzelschreiber* and *Der Meineidbauer*,
have a strong realistic tendency. He also wrote a
series of "Village Tales" and two powerful novels,
Der Schandfleck and *Der Sternsteinhof*. Following
closely in the steps of Anzengruber is PETER ROSEG-
GER (b. 1843), whose prolific writings picture Styrian
landscape and Styrian folk. He makes his characters a part of their environment, and charms us by
the simplicity of his diction as well as by his broad
sympathy and ability to interpret human nature.
His best known works are *Die Schriften des Wald-
schulmeisters* and *Das ewige Licht*.

CHARLES SEALSFIELD, whose real name was Karl
Anton Postl, and FRIEDRICH GERSTÄCKER wrote
about America, but their novels have not been appreciated, except perhaps Gerstäcker's *Germels-
hausen*, which gives a delightful picture of a German
village. As writers of antiquarian novels, FELIX
DAHN (b. 1834) and GEORG EBERS (1837–98) show
a more didactic spirit; the former is well known by
his novel *Ein Kampf um Rom*, and the latter, a noted
Egyptologist, by *Uarda*, *Homo sum*, and the sentimental novel *Eine ägyptische Königstochter*.

The greatest novelist of this age is the Swiss GOTT-
FRIED KELLER (1819–90), who first attracted attention by a sort of autobiographical romance, *Der grüne*

Heinrich, which was soon followed by a volume of novelettes, *Die Leute von Seldwyla.* Two novels of this collection, *Romeo und Julia auf dem Dorfe* and *Kleider machen Leute,* have become very popular. Another collection of novels, *Sieben Legenden,* appeared in 1872, and six years later a third collection under the title *Züricher Novellen,* among which *Das Fähnlein der sieben Aufrechten* and *Der Landvogt von Greifensee* show Keller's humor and mastery of prose fiction. His last novel, *Martin Salander,* written in 1886, was too prosaic to become popular. Keller was possessed of true artistic gifts, good common sense, and strong patriotism, and has been rightly called the "Shakespeare of the German short story."

Another Swiss writer of considerable note is CONRAD FERDINAND MEYER (1825–98), whose works are characterized by beauty of style and form, subtle wit, and perfect skill in scenic descriptions. His first novel, *Jürg Jenatsch,* gives a good example of Swiss patriotism. *Der Heilige* relates the story of Thomas à Becket and *Das Amulett* describes the awful massacre of St. Bartholomew. *Gustav Adolfs Page, Die Versuchung des Pescara,* and *Angela Borgia* are also historical in character. Besides other historical novelettes, and a small book of poems, Meyer wrote a good epic, *Huttens letzte Tage.*

A popular writer of short stories is THEODOR STORM (1817–88). His writings are marked by a love of home and nature, sweetness of language, and tenderness of sentiment. He has a fondness for reminiscence, and his best novels reveal an undertone of sadness and resignation. The traces of Romantic influence found in his earlier novels, *Im Sonnenschein, Ein grünes Blatt*, and in his best known story, *Immensee*, are less pronounced in *Psyche*, and in his later stories, *In St. Jürgen, Carsten Curator, Viola Tricolor*, and *Pole Poppenspäler*, which show a healthy realism and a more positive individuality. Storm also published some *Gedichte* (1853), which give him a place as a lyric poet of note.

A writer who has had many imitators is JOSEPH VICTOR VON SCHEFFEL (1826–86), author of the popular epic *Der Trompeter von Säkkingen*. Scheffel is decidedly German in thought and feeling, and his works reflect the taste and the ideals of his time. Patriotic and genial, he, more than any other modern writer, has revived the old Teutonic spirit, which may account to some extent for his great popularity among the German people. In his younger years Scheffel wrote many humorous student songs, which he collected, and very reluctantly published, under the title of *Gaudeamus*, in 1867. His best work is the historical romance *Ekkehard, eine Geschichte aus dem zehnten Jahrhundert*. The enthusiastic celebration of his fiftieth birthday in all parts of Germany demonstrates how greatly his works have been appreciated by his people.

Foremost among his numerous followers are JULIUS WOLFF (b. 1834), who wrote *Der Ratten-jänger von Hameln*, *Der wilde Jäger*, and *Tann-häuser*, and RUDOLF BAUMBACH (b. 1840), whose *Lieder eines fahrenden Gesellen* reveal a kinship to Scheffel's sentimental lyrics, whom he resembles, also, in his love for his Fatherland, and his strong Roman-tic tendency. But it is as a delineator of Thuringian village life that Baumbach most appeals to his read-ers. His keen sense of humor, simplicity of form, and tender pathos have made his stories popular. Among his best productions are *Zlatorog*, an Alpine saga, *Horand und Hilde*, *Der Schwiegersohn*, *Frau Holde*, and *Das Habichtsfräulein*.

The most productive writer of this period is PAUL HEYSE (b. 1830), whose works have been published in twenty-nine volumes, containing poems, tales, dramas, and novels. He has also translated several volumes of Spanish and Italian literature. In the drama he has been only moderately successful, but as a writer of short stories he is without a rival. His style is graphic and simple, and shows remarkable artistic sense and perfection. His portrayal of Italian characters is especially good, being true to life and full of vigorous action. *L'Arrabbiata* is in this re-spect unsurpassed. Other novels well known to American students of German are *Das Mädchen von Treppi*, *Die Hochzeit auf Capri*, *Anfang und Ende*, *Die Einsamen*, and *Die Blinden*. His more ambitious novels, like *Kinder der Welt* and *Im Paradiese*, show traces of pessimism and a lack of form and sincerity. Heyse was called to Munich by Maximilian II in 1854, where another talented writer of short stories, WILHELM H. RIEHL (1823–97), became celebrated for his realistic and vivid allusions to the political and social conditions of Germany's past. His "Novellen" are well written and of a high moral standard. He is best known by his *Kulturgeschichtliche Novellen.* Especially entertaining are such stories as *Der Fluch der Schönheit, Das Spielmannskind, Der stumme Ratsherr*, and *Burg Neideck.*

Two North Germans, WILHELM JENSEN and ADOLF WILBRANDT, both born in 1837, imitate the Munich writers in thought and style. The former is the author of the beautiful prose idyl *Die braune Erica;* the latter is more successful as a novelist than as a dramatist. His *Jugendliebe* and *Der Meister von Palmyra* are read in our schools to-day.

Among the women writers who attracted considerable attention in the nineteenth century is ANNETTE VON DROSTE-HÜLSHOFF (1797–1848), who is without doubt the greatest poetess Germany has produced. She was fond of nature, which she beautifully describes in the cycle of *Haidebilder*, and her religious poems are equal to those written during the Reformation Period. She discards all sentimentality, lacks consideration for her readers, and inclines toward pessimism.

Fiction is ably represented by the two eminent women GRÄFIN IDA HAHN-HAHN and FANNY LE-WALD. Both show in their writings the influence of "Young Germany." In her collection of novels *Aus der Gesellschaft*, Hahn-Hahn delights in portraying aristocratic society; Fanny Lewald, while trying to solve the same problems of society, is more practical and reasonable, and may be considered the early champion of the "new woman." LUISE MÜHLBACH became known by her historical romances, and WILHELMINE VON HILLERN by her story *Höher als die Kirche*. E. MARLITT, whose real name is Eugenie John, gained popularity by her novels *Goldelse*, *Reichsgräfin Gisela*, *Das Geheimnis der alten Mamsell*, and others, which have been translated into English.

The Austrian MARIE VON EBNER-ESCHENBACH (b. 1830) is recognized as one of the best of the short story writers. In *Die Freiherren von Gemperlein* she reveals her wit and satire in depicting aristocratic life in Austria. Representatives of the woman's cause are GABRIELE REUTER and HELENE BÖHLAU. Other writers worthy of mention are CARMEN SYLVA, the queen of Roumania, BETTY PAOLI, OTTILIE WILDER-MUTH, CLARA VIEBIG, and RICARDA HUCH.

To the latter part of this period belong the humorists WILHELM RAABE, WILHELM BUSCH, and HEINRICH SEIDEL. Raabe is not very well known, except in Germany, where he first attracted attention

by the charming idyl *Die Chronik der Sperlingsgasse,*
which was followed by many stories after the manner
and style of Jean Paul. Busch is known by *Max und
Moritz* and *Die fromme Helene,* and Seidel by his
inimitable *Leberecht Hühnchen* (1882), which never
fails to interest the reader by its graceful style and
delightful humor.

In the decade which followed the Franco-Prussian
War, the stern historical spirit of Germany was represented by ERNST VON WILDENBRUCH (1845–1908),
who, after writing *Lieder und Balladen,* turned his
attention to the historical drama. His tragedy *Die
Karolinger* was received with great enthusiasm in
Berlin in 1881. Plays followed in rapid succession,
and in 1884 he was awarded the Schiller prize for
superior work. *Christoph Marlow* (1884) and *Das
neue Gebot* (1886) mark an advance in dramatic
skill, while *Die Quitzows* (1888), although more
faulty in structure, was a great success on the stage.
Der Generalfeldoberst (1889) and *Der neue Herr*
(1891) give vivid historical pictures and portray
accurately the real life of the common people. With
the double tragedy *Heinrich und Heinrichs Ge-
schlecht* Wildenbruch scored a great success, and received the double Schiller prize. His reputation was
further augmented by *Die Tochter des Erasmus*
(1898), a Reformation drama. Later in life Wildenbruch returned to fiction and produced such interesting and pathetical stories as *Der Letzte* and

Das edle Blut. Among his other numerous stories are *Der Meister von Tanagra, Eifernde Liebe, Die heilige Frau,* and *Die Schwesterseele.*

THEODOR FONTANE (1819–98), although of French parentage, was born at Neuruppin in the Mark of Brandenburg. His first historical romance, *Vor dem Sturm* (1878), shows the influence of Willibald Alexis, but Fontane gradually worked his way towards a realistic style, and proved himself the forerunner of the modern German novel by his publication of *L'Adultera* in 1882. *Effi Briest* (1895) which depicts life and scenes in the Mark of Brandenburg, is perhaps his best work.

Another native of North Germany, and a very talented poet, was DETLEV VON LILIENCRON (1844–1909). He wrote several dramas and other prose works, but his fame rests upon his lyrics, the first collection of which *Adjutantenritte und andere Gedichte* was published in 1883.

At the close of the nineteenth century the writings of FRIEDRICH W. NIETZSCHE, the poet-philosopher, voiced the feelings of the younger generation of writers, to whom the teachings of Schopenhauer and the spirit of Hegelianism had become distasteful, and advocated a more optimistic "Weltanschauung." At this time German literature also came again under foreign influence as in the Storm and Stress period, which resulted in the realistic movement. Zola in France, Ibsen in Scandinavia, and Tolstoy in Russia were the recognized leaders of the movement and were followed in Germany by HAUPTMANN and HERMANN SUDERMANN (b. 1857). The new movement represents a struggle between realism and idealism, and affects the drama more than the novel. Sudermann, an East Prussian, is a novelist and dramatist who has, to a large extent, taken his models from the foreign modern naturalistic schools. In 1887 he published a collection of short stories under the title *Im Zwielicht*, and also his first work of real importance, *Frau Sorge*, one of the greatest modern German novels. These works were followed by two short tales, *Die Geschwister*, in 1888, and *Der Katzensteg*, considered his finest work of fiction, in 1889. Sudermann's longest novel, *Es war*, appeared in 1894, but it was written ten years earlier, which may account in a measure for some of its defects. While his novels are written in simple German, and touch all phases of human experiences, his main fault lies in the too elaborate delineation of his characters. But it is as a dramatist that Sudermann has gained well-merited fame. His first drama, *Die Ehre* (1889), at once attracted the attention of all Germany, and revealed him as a dramatist of great force and skill. His next play, *Sodoms Ende* (1891), a satire on false ideas of honor, was less successful. In *Heimat* (1893), known also as *Magda*, the author treats the dramatic motive of *Die Ehre* from a different standpoint. This is Sudermann's most popular play. The somewhat grim comedy *Die Schmetterlingsschlacht* (1895) was followed by his resignation tragedy *Das Glück im Winkel* (1895), which did not meet with the success it deserved. *Morituri* (1897) is a collection of three one-act plays, *Teja, Fritzchen,* and *Das Ewig-Männliche,* each picturing the feelings of a man in different ages of civilization, conscious of the approach of death. *Johannes* (1898) has a biblical hero with a modern background. His next play, *Die drei Reiherfedern* (1898), is of an entirely different stamp and may be called a "Märchendrama." In the later dramas *Johannisfeuer* (1900) and *Es lebe das Leben* (1902), the author again concerns himself with social problems. The comedy *Der Sturmgeselle Sokrates* (1903) and *Das Blumenboot* (1905), a four-act drama, are not up to the high standard of his former works. Sudermann's novels, as well as his dramas, show a dramatic quality, simplicity of art, skill in depicting scenes, courage of conviction, and a broad treatment of the social problems of his time not to be found in any other writer.

The second and most original writer of the realistic school is GERHART HAUPTMANN (b. 1862) a Silesian, considered by some the greatest literary man in Germany to-day. He is the first German man of letters upon whom Oxford has conferred the degree of LL.D. His first poetic publication, *Promethidenlos* (1885), is modeled on Byron's *Childe Harold* while *Vor Sonnenaufgang* (1889), *Das Friedensfest* (1890), and *Einsame Menschen* (1891) show the influence of Zola, Tolstoy, and Ibsen. But his rare dramatic power is better revealed in the naturalistic tragedy *Die Weber* (1892), which portrays the physical distress of the Silesian weavers, and their revolt against oppression. This work attracted much attention and made its author popular. His next drama, *Kollege Crampton* (1892), the story of a painter who has fallen into evil ways, and *Der Biberpelz* (1893), a comedy of provincial life, were also well received, and show Hauptmann's skill in accurate *milieu* painting. Idealism is blended with realism in the unique and pathetic play *Hanneles Himmelfahrt* (1893), which was a remarkable success, but the historical tragedy *Florian Geyer* (1895), which takes us back to the restless time of Götz von Berlichingen, was a complete failure. In 1897 appeared the "Märchendrama" *Die versunkene Glocke*, which attracted unprecedented attention in Germany and passed through more than fifty editions, but in America it met with a cool reception on the stage. Symbolism, allegory, and realistic features are pleasingly intermingled, and easily interpreted. Hauptmann's next drama, *Fuhrmann Henschel* (1898), was written in the Silesian dialect, like *Die Weber*, and marks a return to the realistic method of his earlier dramas. It is considered one of the greatest peasant tragedies ever written, and found many

imitators in Germany. The prologue of Shakespeare's *Taming of the Shrew* gave Hauptmann the
idea for the tramp-comedy *Schluck und Jau* (1900).
In this same year *Michael Kramer*, the story of an
artist who just fell short of greatness, was written,
and although lacking in dramatic action its characters are attractive and well depicted. The tragi-
comedy *Der rote Hahn*, a companion piece to *Der
Biberpelz*, appeared in the following year. Not
quite up to his high standard of excellence is *Der
arme Heinrich* (1902), which resembles very much
the mediaeval epic of the same name by Hartmann
von Aue. Hauptmann's admirers were again disappointed when the five-act drama, *Rose Bernd*, appeared in 1903. *Elga*, a family drama, was written
in 1906, and is based on one of Grillparzer's novels.
His latest work is *Kaiser Karls Geisel* (1908). In
spite of the many defects to be found in Hauptmann's
works, we must give him the place of honor among
the greatest writers in Germany to-day.

The German theater has been provided, also, with
plays by minor dramatists, which have reflected
great credit on the literary activity of modern Germany. MAX HALBE (b. 1865), has contributed the
two interesting plays, *Jugend* (1893) and *Mutter
Erde* (1898); and LUDWIG FULDA (b. 1862) has
added several dramas after the models of his predecessors. The little comedy *Die Aufrichtigen* first
brought him into notice as an original writer. Be-

sides publishing translations he has produced some important plays which have met with considerable success on the stage. In his three-act play *Das verlorene Paradies* (1890), he shows superiority in many respects over his models, *Frau Sorge* and *Die Ehre*. His most popular work is *Der Talisman* (1893), while *Der Sohn des Kalifen* (1897) is perhaps his best. His more recent dramas betray many weaknesses, but reveal considerable refinement of diction and exquisite humor. His latest comedy is *Der Dummkopf*.

Among other representative contemporaries whose realistic writings have attracted attention are O. E. HARTLEBEN (b. 1864), KARL BLEIBTREU (b. 1859), M. KRETZER (b. 1854), K. ALBERTI (b. 1862), and the Austrian writers A. SCHNITZLER (b. 1862), H. BAHR (b. 1863), and H. VON HOFMANNSTHAL (b. 1874).

Although the period after the Revolution of 1848 has been characterized by pessimism, the period since the Franco-Prussian War has witnessed a new awakening of the national spirit, and we believe this revival of literary interest at the close of the nineteenth century and at the beginning of the twentieth is indicative of a still greater and grander development in German literature.

APPENDIX

THE GERMAN EMPIRE

THE German Empire has existed in its present
political condition since 1871. It embraces the central part of Europe, and is therefore in close touch
with Russia, Austria-Hungary, France, Belgium, the
Netherlands, Denmark, and Great Britain. Its area
is 208,830 square miles, while its colonies comprise
a territory about five times as large as the empire
itself. It extends 750 miles east and west, and about
600 miles north and south, and has a sea frontage
of about 1,200 miles. According to the statistics of
1905, it ranks fourth in population (60,641,278), and
second in size among the countries of Europe. Germany presents two distinct physical formations: the
northern part is lowland, while the central and southern portions are highland, giving a diversity of scenery,—snow-capped highlands, wooded hills, sandy
plains, and fertile valleys. Except the Danube,
its most important streams flow north and empty
into the North and Baltic Seas. The Rhine belongs
to three countries, Switzerland, Germany, and the

Netherlands, and is commercially the most important river of Germany. Its most picturesque scenery is to be found between Coblenz and Mainz. The largest ports on the North Sea are Hamburg on the Elbe, and Bremen on the Weser; the Baltic ports are Stettin, Danzig, Kiel, and Lübeck. The most northern mountain system, beginning in the east with the Sudetic Mountains, and including the Riesengebirge, Erzgebirge, Fichtelgebirge, and Thuringian Forest, with the Harz Mountains a little to the north, extends through the middle of Germany in a general east and west direction, and forms the boundary between North and South Germany. The Taunus, in the west, is surrounded by one of the best wine regions of Germany, and farther south along the opposite bank of the Rhine rise the Vosges Mountains. In the south are the Swabian and Franconian Jura, the Black Forest, and the Tyrolese Alps. The Zugspitze, in Bavaria, 9,725 feet high, is the highest mountain. Germany is especially rich in mineral springs, the most noted of which are Baden-Baden, Kissingen, Wiesbaden, Homburg, and Ems. The climate is less diversified than might be expected, the greater heat of the more southern latitudes being modified by the Alps, and the ocean counteracts the cold of the north. The Rhinelands, the Moselle, Main, and Neckar valleys have the most attractive climate, while the south slope of the Taunus produces excellent wines, almonds, and chestnuts.

Maize is grown in the fertile valleys of the Rhine and the Neckar, but rye is the chief cereal cultivated for food.

Until about the middle of the last century Germany was chiefly an agricultural nation, but with the establishment of internal free trade (Zollverein, 1833) many of the barriers to commerce were removed and Germany rose to the front rank as an industrial and commercial power.

In drugs and other chemical products Germany almost controls the markets of the world, having nearly seven hundred factories. The manufacture of colors has been carried to great perfection. Essen, Bochum, and Witten are noted for their steel works, the largest establishment being that of Krupp at Essen, famous for its cannon. Among the porcelain factories the one at Meissen (established 1710) is the oldest and most famous. The so-called Dresden china comes from this factory. Silks and velvets are manufactured chiefly in Rhenish Prussia.

With one of the most extensive railway systems in the world, owned largely by the various state governments, with a postal department which collects and delivers mail matter more frequently in its large cities than is the case in our own country, with the telephone and telegraph managed by the German postal authorities, and with her high grade commercial and technical schools, Germany offers superior opportunities for the development of all her industries.

GOVERNMENT

The German Empire is governed according to the Constitution of April 16, 1871. It consists of four kingdoms, six grand duchies, five duchies, seven principalities, and three free cities, in all twenty-five states and one Imperial Territory, under the King of Prussia, William II., to whom belongs also the title of German Emperor.

KINGDOMS	GRAND DUCHIES	DUCHIES
Prussia	Baden	Brunswick
Bavaria	Hesse	Saxe-Meiningen
Saxony	Mecklenburg-Schwerin	Saxe-Altenburg
Württemberg	Saxe-Weimar	Saxe-Coburg-Gotha
	Mecklenburg-Strelitz	Anhalt
	Oldenburg	

PRINCIPALITIES	FREE CITIES	IMPERIAL TERRITORY
Schwarzburg-Rudolstadt	Lübeck	Alsace-Lorraine
Schwarzburg-Sondershausen	Bremen	
Waldeck	Hamburg	
Reuss (elder line)		
Reuss (younger line)		
Schaumburg-Lippe		
Lippe		

According to the Constitution the legislative and the executive power is vested in the Emperor, the Federal Council (Bundesrat), and the National Parliament (Reichstag). The Emperor is chief commander of the military and naval forces; he represents the Empire in all its dealings with foreign countries, appoints and receives ambassadors and consuls, appoints the Imperial Chancellor, and removes him at will, and declares war and makes peace; but he has no veto power such as the President of the United States possesses.

BUNDESRAT. The Constitution determines that there shall be fifty-eight votes in the Bundesrat, of which seventeen fall to Prussia. The members are appointed by the several states, and must vote as instructed by their respective governments. The Bundesrat meets annually in Berlin, and sits with closed doors. No man can be a member of the Bundesrat and of the Reichstag at the same time. This body can assemble without the Reichstag, but the latter can convene only while the Bundesrat is in session. The Chancellor of the Empire, or his substitute, is president of this council, whose functions are nearly as important as those of the Emperor, being not only legislative, but administrative as well.

REICHSTAG. While the Bundesrat represents the individual states, the Reichstag represents the nation as a whole,—the people. It is composed of 397 members, elected by universal suffrage. Prussia alone has about 236, or three fifths of the whole number. The Emperor calls the Reichstag together, and dismisses it; in case of dismissal new elections must be held within sixty days, and it must reassemble within ninety days of its dissolution. The Reichstag meets annually, and its members, as such, receive no pay, and are uninstructed. This body not only treats petitions submitted to it, but may also propose measures and ask that the Bundesrat act upon them. But all important bills are carefully prepared and passed by the Bundesrat before they reach the Reichstag. Generally speaking, the code of parliamentary rules governing the Reichstag is neither so exacting nor so comprehensive as in our House of Representatives. The sessions are uninteresting on account of the general absence of oratory and wit. The Germans are naturally slow and phlegmatic, yet there are men, like August Bebel, the Socialist veteran, who stir the Reichstag by their fluent and convincing speeches.

ARMY AND NAVY

The German army of to-day is, as it has been from earliest times, "a people in arms." Even in the tenth century the words *army* and *navy* were synonymous among the Saxons. The army is the very life of the people; and Germany can have peace, and exist as a nation only so long as she is well prepared for war.

Nowhere else in the world is the army so closely related to the nation, and nowhere else is the confidence in the army greater, nor any insult to it more keenly felt than among the Germans. Aroused by such poets as Arndt, Körner, and Schenkendorf, and led by such military leaders as Scharnhorst, Gneisenau, Blücher, and von Bülow, Germany was able to throw off the yoke of Napoleon in the War of Liberation in 1813, and the soldier could no longer be considered a mercenary, as in the Thirty Years' War. During the peaceful years which followed, very little was done to develop and increase the fighting force, until King William of Prussia, feeling his inability to cope with his neighbors, began the reorganization of the army with the aid of Bismarck, Roon, and von Moltke.

The splendid results of 1866 and 1871 tell the story of their labors to unite all Germany, and make the army irresistible. Out of this union of the different states against a common foe came forth the present powerful German army. What the fathers have obtained through bloody conflicts, the sons must preserve as a sacred heritage. The army of to-day is, without doubt, the most efficient fighting force in the world, and has served as a model for the armies of many other countries. In time of peace the armed forces of Prussia, Bavaria, and the other states are each under command of the sovereign of the state; but the German Emperor, William II., becomes in time of war commander in chief of the army, which numbers more than 10,000,000 soldiers,—or an army eight times larger than the Japanese army which defeated the Russians in the late war. Germany produces about 250,000 trained soldiers every year.

Every male German, unless physically incapacitated, owes military service from the end of his twentieth, to the completion of his thirty-ninth year.

Within this period seven years must be passed in the active army, two in actual service (three for cavalry and artillery), and the rest in the reserve. The next twelve years are passed in the LANDWEHR; and so long as he is enrolled in the reserve, or the first ban of the Landwehr, the citizen is liable to be called into camp every year for a few weeks.

The LANDSTURM consists of all Germans from the end of the seventeenth to the end of the forty-fifth year who are not enrolled in any of the above mentioned bodies. The Landwehr of the second ban and the Landsturm are summoned only in time of war.

Young men over seventeen years of age, who volunteer for active service, pass an examination on general subjects, and agree to equip and maintain themselves while in service, are admitted into the reserve after one year's service. This privilege is also granted to teachers.

The present total peace establishment of the German army is 629,508 men exclusive of reserves of Landwehr and Landsturm. While the army is provided with permanent officers, the body of private soldiers is constantly changing. The period of service for the infantry with the colors is two years, for the artillery and cavalry three years. Students who are able to pay for their own maintenance and equipment, called "volunteers," need serve but one year with the colors. These years of service are no child's play for the young German. No training can make him more willing to serve the land that gave him birth, nor better develop his character, broaden him educationally, teach him self-denial, and inform him concerning the resources of his country, its traffic, citizenship, and institutions, than these years of service in the army. Professor Münsterberg has well said: "The years in the army constitute a national school-time which keeps body and soul in strength and vigor."

The German navy is to-day virtually under the jurisdiction of the Emperor, who may be said to have recreated the German fleet, so that it now ranks third among the great powers of the world. The present personnel consists of 2,315 officers, and 44,432 men. Service in the navy, except in the case of officers, is unpaid, and is regarded, as in the army, a civic duty. This service is not burdensome, and nowhere will you find a better system of training, a more enthusiastic spirit animating men, and more efficient officers than in the German navy. The Kaiser Wilhelm Canal makes it possible for large vessels to reach the North Sea from the Baltic, and is a favorable refuge in case of necessity.

THE IMPERIAL FAMILY

The reigning family of Germany is descended from Frederick von Hohenzollern (980), and Frederick William the Elector of Brandenburg (1688), whose son became King of Prussia. Since January 18, 1871, the House of Hohenzollern has been vested with the dignity of German Emperor. William I. was the son of Frederick William III., and the much beloved Queen Louise. Simple in tastes, straightforward in character, he combined all the sterling qualities of true Germanic manhood. In him was found a force for shaping the destiny of the nation; in him the Germanic dream of national unity was to be realized. He discerned the noble character and strength of his people, and they in turn learned to appreciate the grand old man, so that at the age of ninety he was idolized by the whole nation, whose feelings are expressed in these words: "His Majesty, our most gracious Kaiser, and victorious leader in numerous battles, the unifier of Germany's princes and people, the father of his country, and custodian of the peace of Europe, the creator of a new ideal world; long may he live!" William I. was succeeded by his son Frederick III., who was doomed to reign but a few months. The nation looked to him for a reconciliation of the differences still existing in the Fatherland. He was the purest embodiment of all that is noble in German character; and yet many feared that had he lived his goodness would have been abused and his trust misplaced, for he lacked that firmness which is essential to guide national affairs in troublesome times. His kindly disposition, affable manners, cosmopolitan breadth, and sympathy made him very popular. The present emperor, William II., succeeded to the throne at the death of his father in 1888. He was born January 27, 1859. He married the Princess Victoria of Schleswig-Holstein, an excellent woman and several months his senior. Following the old ideal of a German housewife she is devoted to the three K's: "Kirche," "Küche" and "Kinder." They have seven children, Frederick William (the Crown Prince), William Eitel-Frederick, Adalbert, August, Oscar, Joachim, and Victoria Louise. The Emperor is an indefatigable worker and prefers the conversation of brilliant men to books. In politics he is more like his grandfather, an autocrat, who believes in the divine right of kings. He knows all that is going on in the world and has a high conception of what a ruler should be. Being of a nervous temperament, he often acts hastily and sometimes unwisely. He seems to think it his prerogative and duty not only to shape the foreign policy of Germany, and to influence the army and navy, but also to control the press and pulpit, and the arts and sciences. He fears and dislikes the rising Socialist party, which he considers "a horde of men unworthy to bear the name of Germans." He is, without doubt, the most misunderstood of all the Hohenzollerns, for about none of his predecessors has public opinion so wavered. Some of his people are extremely optimistic with regard to what may be expected of him, while others distrust him on account of his warlike proclivities. Be this as it may, the Emperor is in a very difficult position and we are inclined to believe that he has justified a flattering estimate of his character.

CHANCELLORS OF THE EMPIRE

OTTO EDUARD LEOPOLD PRINCE VON BISMARCK, the so-called Iron Chancellor, was the first Chancellor of the German Empire. When William I. succeeded Frederick William IV. to the Prussian throne, Bismarck was made head of the Prussian Cabinet and Minister of Foreign Affairs. He worked for the unification of Germany under Prussian leadership, and strove to place the new Empire in the forefront of European nations. After the Franco-German war he organized the internal affairs of Germany upon a new basis and developed an imperial policy of the first rank. He did much to stimulate industry and thereby to check the continuous emigration from Germany. Although a man of strong passions, he always sought to maintain peace. After the Emperor's death in 1888, Bismarck continued in office during the brief reign of Emperor Frederick. When William II. succeeded to the throne, Bismarck found he had to deal with a young, headstrong, and autocratic ruler. After numerous quarrels Bismarck resigned on March 20, 1890. He was without doubt one of the greatest statesmen of all time. He died July 30, 1898.

GEORG LEO, COUNT VON CAPRIVI, distinguished himself as a member of the general staff of the First Army Corps. Through the influence of Bismarck he became the Chief of the Admiralty, and in this capacity reorganized the navy upon its present basis. In March, 1890, he succeeded Bismarck as Chancellor, and President of the Prussian Ministry. His position was a trying and difficult one, but he showed great fortitude and ability in the administration of the affairs of the restless William II. He resigned in 1894, and died February 6, 1899. His leading characteristics were good common sense, obedience and loyalty to the Emperor, and simple modes of speech and living. He must be credited with the commercial prosperity and expansion which Germany enjoyed for a decade. He was liberal in his political and social ideas, and the most accessible Chancellor Germany has ever had.

FRIEDRICH LUDWIG, PRINCE VON HOHENLOHE, a man of rare endowment as a leader and a soldier, was the successor of Chancellor Caprivi. He was a representative of South Germany, being governor of Alsace-Lorraine, when created Imperial Chancellor in 1894. His efforts in behalf of a united Germany were greatly appreciated. He was highly favored by the Emperor, whose colonial policy and ideas for a powerful navy he assiduously fostered. In his economic convictions he was very much like Caprivi, and he favored a close commercial treaty with the

United States. He was hindered in the full exercise of his powers by the infirmities of old age, so that during the last year of his service his duties were discharged by Count von Bülow, who was during the next year appointed to succeed him. Von Hohenlohe resigned in 1900, and died July 6, 1901.

BERNHARD, PRINCE VON BÜLOW succeeded Count von Hohenlohe in 1900. He is to be classed among the ablest men of Germany to-day. After serving with considerable distinction in the war of 1871, he represented his country in diplomatic service abroad until he became Chancellor of the German Empire and Prime Minister of Prussia in 1900. He seemed to be held in high esteem by the Emperor and favored imperial expansion. Like his predecessor he also favored a better political understanding between Germany and the United States. Although he may at times have appeared unstable and enigmatical, he nevertheless was a strong advocate of peace and prosperity.

He resigned July 14, 1909, and was succeeded by THEOBALD VON BETHMANN-HOLLWEG, a man of reserved and thoughtful habits, who has been called the "Philosopher Statesman." He is fifty-three years old, possesses an excellent knowledge of the English language, and is well versed in American affairs. In politics he is a mild Conservative, but he applies to himself the traditional policy that the servants of the crown must be non-partisan.

The German Language

The Germanic languages are descended from the Indo-European family, to which the Sanskrit, Persian, Slavonic, Celtic, Greek, and Latin belong, and are divided into three groups. To the first, East Germanic, belongs Gothic, which is nearly akin to English and German, but which has completely died out. Manuscripts which contain fragments of the translation of the Bible are the only source of our knowledge of the Gothic language. The second group, the North Germanic, includes the Scandinavian languages: Icelandic, Danish-Norwegian, and Swedish. The West Germanic forms the third group and lives on in the Low German which embraces the English and Dutch, and in the High German which is spoken in Germany, Switzerland, in certain provinces of Austria-Hungary, and in parts of the New World. The history of the development of the High German may be conveniently divided into the following three periods:

1. Old High German begins with the sixth century, and continues to the end of the eleventh. It was spoken mostly in the south and is characterized by full vowels in final syllables.

2. Middle High German extends from the eleventh to the middle of the fourteenth century. In this period the language has spread to the middle of Germany and become the official language. The weakening of the full vowels to *e*, and the more ex-

tended use of the umlaut are the principal differences of the OHG. and MHG. periods.

3. New High German continues from the close of the MHG. period to the present, and may be divided into the following divisions: (a) the *pre-classical*, which reaches to the middle of the eighteenth century and contains the Saxonic translation of the Bible by Luther, who was instrumental in spreading and developing the language which became the basis of modern German; (b) the *classical*, represented by the great writers, Lessing, Schiller, and Goethe, and (c) the *post-classical*, which may be said to extend from Schiller's death to the present.   Throughout this entire period, the language has suffered many changes by shortening words, simplifying the grammar, eliminating foreign words, and adopting a uniform *Schriftsprache* as far as possible.

The German language abounds in dialects, and almost every large city and province has its own peculiar manner of speech.   We may, however, divide the dialects into four groups: Low German, Upper German, Franconian, and Middle German.

1. Low German (Plattdeutsch) is a group of dialects spoken in the northern provinces of Germany.

2. Upper German is spoken in Switzerland, Alsace, South Baden, Swabia, Bavaria, and certain provinces in Austria.

3. Franconian is divided into Upper Franconian, which includes East Franconian and Rhenish Fran-

conian, and Middle Franconian, which embraces the
territory along the Moselle and along the Rhine from
Coblenz to Düsseldorf.

4. East Middle German includes Silesia, Upper
Saxony, and Thuringia.

EDUCATION

No people have taken more thought and pains to
develop a typical educational system than the Germans. Although there is no absolute uniformity
in the school systems of the various German states
on account of political and religious differences,
they nevertheless resemble parts of a highly organized machine, every part of which is related to the
other. The Prussian school system is usually taken
as the standard. In this state the schools are classed
as follows: *Kindergarten*, which are privately conducted; *Volksschulen*, or elementary schools, which
provide for the entire period of compulsory attend-
ance of pupils under fourteen years of age; *Bürgerschulen*, or middle schools of a higher grade; and
Höhere Bürgerschulen, which in some parts of Germany are not included with the secondary schools.
Besides these schools there are the more advanced
Gymnasien, with nine-year courses, to attend which
pupils must be nine years of age; *Progymnasien*,
with six or seven-year courses, usually lacking some
of the higher classes and located in the smaller
towns; *Realgymnasien*, with nine-year courses, includ-

ing Latin; *Realprogymnasien*, with six-year courses, including Latin; *Oberrealschulen*, with nine-year courses, without Latin; *Realschulen*, with six-year courses, without Latin. The aim of the Gymnasium is, "to prepare its students through a broad humanistic training for the independent study of the arts and sciences." It is the classical preparatory school for the university and requires of the pupil for entrance a three-years' preparatory course in reading, writing, arithmetic, and religion. This preparation may be had in the elementary schools, private and public, and in the Vorschulen connected with the Gymnasien. The Progymnasien are merely Gymnasien having, as a rule, only the lower and middle classes. The aim of the Realgymnasium "is to give the youth a liberal education, founded, however, especially on instruction in the modern languages, mathematics, and the natural sciences." The curriculum corresponds to the course of study of the American High School, and graduates are admitted to university courses in mathematics, the natural sciences, and modern languages, and to all technological schools, but are denied admission to the professions of law, medicine, and theology, and to certain positions in the state. There are about 56,560 schools in all, maintained at a cost of sixty millions annually, and the number of illiterates is very small, since ninety-nine per cent. of all adults in Germany can read and write.

Included in the above number of schools are 128 Realgymnasien and 93 Realprogymnasien. The former "aim to fit their students for more effectual and intelligent participation in the actual business affairs of life, and therefore place particular emphasis on the modern languages and the natural sciences." The Oberrealschulen have nine-year courses, while the Realschulen have six. Graduates of the latter are well prepared to take up the duties of practical life and are on a par with the graduates of the former. Coeducation is restricted to the Volksschulen, where the boys occupy one end of the building and the girls the other. There are, however, *Höhere Mädchenschulen*, which have a nine years' course and are of the same grade as the Gymnasien. The higher education of girls is left to private institutions. Some universities allow women to continue their studies, and grant them the degree of Ph.D., while others do not admit them at all, or only as "auditors." The German universities have, without doubt, reached a high state of perfection and serve as models for other countries. They are the recognized medium of admission to all the learned professions and all important positions in the civil service. The watchwords of the German university system are, "Lehrfreiheit" and "Lernfreiheit." Without any definitely arranged curriculum a student may pass at will from one university to another. Native students are matriculated on presentation of a certificate of graduation from a Gymnasium; foreigners are required to present a university diploma and a passport. The first semester begins about the middle of October and closes in the latter part of March; the second semester opens early in April and ends about the middle of August. A few universities like Jena and Marburg have summer school courses.

There are also good professional and technological schools in Berlin, Hanover, Aix-la-Chapelle, Munich, Dresden, Stuttgart, Darmstadt, Karlsruhe, and Brunswick. Military academies are established in Berlin and Munich; military engineering schools in Berlin, Munich, Potsdam, Erfurt, Cassel, Metz, and elsewhere. The principal naval academy is located at Kiel. There are twenty-one German universities, the oldest of which is Heidelberg, founded in 1386. Each university is made up of four faculties—law, medicine, philosophy, and theology. Professors rank as Ordinary, Extra-Ordinary, Privat-Docenten or authorized lecturers. The matriculation fee is about 20 M., and if a student comes from another university it is 10 M.

ATTENDANCE AT THE GERMAN UNIVERSITIES
SUMMER SEMESTER 1909

Berlin	7194	Freiburg	2760
Bonn	3801	Giessen	1271
Breslau	2347	Göttingen	2239
Erlangen	1158	Greifswald	967

Halle 2310	Marburg 2134
Heidelberg . . . 2171	Munich . . . 6547
Jena 1606	Münster 1760
Kiel 1593	Rostock . . . 743
Königsberg . . . 1293	Strassburg . . . 1935
Leipzig 4581	Tübingen . . . 1921
	Würzburg . . . 1369	

IDIOMATIC EXPRESSIONS

1. Gefälligst. Bitte. *Please.* Erlauben Sie. Wenn es Ihnen gefällig ist. *If you please.*

2. Ich bitte um Verzeihung. Entschuldigen Sie. *I beg your pardon.*

3. Ich danke. *Thanks.* Danke sehr. Danke bestens. *Thanks very much.* Vielen Dank. Besten Dank. *Many thanks.*

4. Bitte, bitte sehr. *Don't mention it.*

5. Kennen Sie Herrn N.? *Do you know Mr. N.?* Ja, er ist mir bekannt. *Yes, I do.* Leider nicht. *No, I am sorry to say.* Er ist mir ganz unbekannt. *I do not know him at all.* Er kommt mir bekannt vor. *I think I know him.*

6. Sind Sie Ihm vorgestellt? *Have you been introduced to him?* Es freut mich sehr, Ihre Bekanntschaft zu machen. Es freut mich sehr, Sie kennen zu lernen. *I am pleased to make your acquaintance.*

7. Auf Wiedersehen! Leben Sie wohl! *Adieu. Good-by, Farewell.*

8. Schöne, angenehme, glückliche Reise! *A pleasant journey.*

9. Vergessen Sie uns nicht! *Don't forget us.* Grüssen Sie mir Herrn N. *Remember me to Mr. N.* Schöne Grüsse an Herrn N. *Give my kind regards to Mr. N.*

10. Prosit! Zur Gesundheit! Zu Ihrem Wohlsein! *Your good health.*

11. Mahlzeit! Gesegnete Mahlzeit! *I hope you will enjoy,* or *have enjoyed your meal!*

12. Es tut mir leid. *I am sorry.* Es ist schade. *It is too bad.*

13. Er hat einen Bock geschossen. *He has made a blunder.*

14. Er lebt in den Tag hinein. *He lives carelessly.*

15. Er konnte nicht umhin. *He could not help.*

16. Zu Pferde. *On horseback.* Zu Fuss. *On foot.*

17. Er lässt es sich sehr sauer werden. *He works very hard.*

18. Er hat mir etwas weiss gemacht. *He has fooled me, pulled the wool over my eyes.*

19. Es geht mich nichts an. *It does not concern me.*

20. Er hat mich im Stich gelassen. *He has left me in the lurch, deserted me.*

21. Lassen Sie sich's schmecken! *I hope you will enjoy your dinner.*

22. Was den Inhalt des Briefes betrifft. *As to the contents of the letter.*

23. Es geht mir jetzt besser. *I am better now.*

24. Mit Sack und Pack. *With bag and baggage.*

25. Es lässt sich nicht ändern. *It can not be helped.*

26. Sie können sich darauf verlassen. *You may depend upon it.*

27. Sie haben gut reden. *It is all very well for you.*

28. Er lässt sich nichts sagen. *He will not take any advice.*

29. Sie kann nicht abkommen. *She can not get away.*

30. Nichts für ungut. *No offense is intended.*

31. Mach' dass du weg kommst! *Hurry along!*

32. Es steckt etwas dahinter. Es geht nicht mit rechten Dingen zu. *There is something wrong about it.*

33. Die Haare stehen ihm zu Berge. *His hair stands on end.*

34. Das hat nichts zu sagen. *That does not matter.*

35. Ich nehme es nicht so genau mit ihm. *I am not so strict with him.*

36. Das kann Ihnen niemand verdenken. *No one can blame you for that.*

37. Das ist mir ganz egal, einerlei. *It is all the same to me.*

38. Das geschieht ihr recht. *It serves her right.*

39. Das will viel heissen. *That is saying a great deal.*

40. Ich kann nichts dafür. *I can not help it.*

41. Er hat unrecht. *He is wrong.*

42. Billets, gefälligst, meine Herrschaften! *Tickets, please, ladies and gentlemen!*

43. Sitzen bleiben! *Keep your seats.*

44. Nach Leipzig umsteigen! *Change for Leipzig.*

45. Alles umsteigen! *Everybody change cars.*

46. Einsteigen! *All aboard!*

47. Ich möchte gern ein Glas Wasser. *I should like a glass of water.*

48. Was unterstehen Sie sich! *How dare you!*

49. Wollen Sie bei mir zu Mittag essen? *Will you have luncheon with me?*

50. Er hat sich zu Grunde gerichtet. *He has ruined himself.*

51. Unter die Haube kommen. *To be married.*

52. Ich habe ihn ins Auge gefasst. *I have measured him with my eye.*

53. Es bleibt mir nichts übrig. *Nothing is left for me.*

54. Er machte sich auf den Weg. *He started,* or *went on his way.*

55. Es will mir nicht einfallen. *It does not occur to me.*

56. Sie ging die Treppe hinan, hinunter. *She went upstairs, downstairs.*

57. Er liegt in den letzten Zügen. *He is breathing his last.*

58. Wir haben den Kürzeren gezogen. *We have been defeated.*

59. Was fällt Ihnen ein? *What do you mean?*

60. Das passt nicht. *That is not at all proper.*

61. Betrachten Sie sich als geohrfeigt. *Consider your ears boxed.*

62. Er fällt mit der Tür ins Haus. *He blunders out.*

63. Das sollte mir einfallen. *You don't catch me.*

64. Keine Widerrede! *Not another word!*

65. Ich bekleide eine Stelle. *I hold a position.*
66. Es kommt auf einen Tag nicht an. *A day more or less does not matter.*
67. Er hat sich aus dem Staub gemacht. *He has run away.*
68. Ich lasse mir das nicht gefallen. *I will not put up with it.*
69. Es ist um ihn geschehen. *He is done for.*
70. Sie hat es aus der Luft gegriffen. *She has coined it.*
71. Sie können ihre Waare nicht an den Mann bringen. *They can not dispose of their goods.*
72. Sie zieht mich gern auf. *She likes to quiz me.*
73. Mir ist dabei übel zu Mute. *I feel very uneasy about it.*
74. An wem ist die Reihe? *Whose turn is it?*
75. Er ist sehr kurz angebunden. *He is very hasty.*
76. Heute über acht Tagen. *A week hence.*
77. Sie muss sich umziehen. *She must change her dress.*
78. Wir wollen es für diesmal gut sein lassen. *For this time we will let it pass.*
79. Wir müssen die Zeche bezahlen. *We must pay the reckoning.*
80. Sollen wir spazieren fahren, gehen? *Shall we take a drive, walk?*
81. Englisch ist mir geläufig. *I am familiar with English.*

82. Er hat mich zum besten gehabt. *He has made fun of me.*

83. Die Hoffnung ist in die Brüche gegangen. *Hope has been shattered.*

84. Wie viel bin ich Ihnen schuldig? *How much do I owe you?*

85. Was darf ich Ihnen anbieten? *What may I offer you?*

86. Bringen Sie noch eine Tasse Kaffee, bitte. *Another cup of coffee, please.*

87. Ich will ihm auf den Zahn fühlen. *I am going to draw him out, get his opinion.*

88. Das lässt sich hören. *That is worth hearing.*

89. Er liess sich das nicht zweimal sagen. *He did not need to be told twice.*

90. Wir wollen es darauf ankommen lassen. *Let us take our chance.*

91. Der Lehrer ist schuld daran. *The teacher is to blame.*

92. Lassen Sie ihm gewähren. *Let him alone.*

93. Es sei dem, wie ihm wolle. *Be it as it may.*

94. Lassen Sie es gut sein. *Never mind.*

95. Versteht sich! *Of course!*

96. Sie sind wieder vernünftig geworden. *You have come to your senses.*

97. Wir sind im Begriff etwas zu tun. *We are about to do something.*

98. Was Sie nicht sagen! *You don't say so!*

99. Nimm dich in acht! *Take care!*

100. Ich bin im stande das zu tun. *I am capable of doing that.*

101. Sie war es wie sie leibte und lebte. *It was she herself.*

102. Aus dem Stegreife reden. *To speak impromptu.*

103. Um wie viel Uhr frühstücken Sie? *At what time do you breakfast?*

104. Wir haben dem Unterricht nicht beiwohnen können. *We have not been able to attend our classes.*

105. Ich bewerbe mich um die Stelle. *I apply for the place.*

106. Wir machen Sie darauf aufmerksam. *We call your attention to it.*

107. Ich weiss weder aus noch ein. *I am in trouble.*

108. Er ist oben, unten. *He is upstairs, downstairs.*

109. Wir haben nichts daran auszusetzen. *We have no fault to find with it.*

110. Er blieb mir damit vom Halse. *He did not trouble me with that.*

111. Er hat sich darüber den Kopf nicht zerbrochen. *He has not troubled his head about it.*

112. Das hält nicht Stich. *That will not hold good.*

113. Sie kommen mir immer in die Queere. *You always cross my plans.*

114. Er tat es aus freien Stücken. *He did it of his own accord.*

115. Er hat einen Korb bekommen. *He has got the mitten. His offer of marriage has been refused.*

116. Man muss ihm auf die Finger sehen. *He must be closely watched.*

117. Was für dummes Zeug faseln Sie! *What nonsense you talk!*

118. Einen über die Achsel ansehen. *To look with disrespect upon a person.*

119. Jemand etwas anheim stellen. *To refer a matter to some one.*

120. Einen anschwärzen; ihn schwarz machen. *To slander a person.*

121. Einem unter die Arme greifen. *To help one out of trouble.*

122. Ein Auge zudrücken. *To pass a mild judgment.*

123. Unter vier Augen. *Between two persons.*

124. Es hat den Ausschlag gegeben. *It has cast the decision.*

125. Einem eins auswischen. *To injure,* or *give one a black eye.*

126. Auf der Bärenhaut liegen. *To be idle* or *lazy.*

127. Sich die Beine nach etwas ablaufen. *To make a great effort for something.*

128. Sie stecken unter einer Decke. *They are in the same boat.*

129. Guter Dinge sein. *To be of good cheer.*

130. Dem will ich es eintränken. *I will get even with him.*

131. Auf eigene Faust. *At one's own risk.*

132. Er hat sich in die Faust gelacht. *He laughed in his sleeve, behind their back.*

133. Etwas aus dem *ff* (= fein, fein) verstehen. *To understand thoroughly.*

134. Es passt wie die Faust aufs Auge. *It fits very poorly.*

135. Nicht viel Federlesens machen. *To make short work of anything.*

136. Feierabend machen. *To cease work in the evening.*

137. Sie leben auf grossem Fusse. *They make a great display.*

138. Einem den Garaus machen. *To kill a person.*

139. Das ist gehüpft wie gesprungen. *There is no difference.*

140. Etwas an die grosse Glocke hängen. *To make a thing publicly known.*

141. Leben wie der liebe Gott in Frankreich. *To take life easy.*

142. Er kommt auf keinen grünen Zweig. *He does not prosper.*

143. Da liegt der Hase im Pfeffer. *Here is the point. Here's the rub.*

144. Ganz aus dem Häuschen sein. *To act very foolishly.*

145. Ich werde es ihm heimzahlen. *I will get even with him.*

146. Etwas in Hülle und Fülle haben. *To have a superabundance.*

147. Er hat Vögel unter dem Hut. *He is too lazy to take off his hat.*

148. Er macht Kalender. *He troubles himself unnecessarily.*

149. Etwas auf die hohe Kant legen. *To be saving.*

150. Er ist kaput. *He is played out.*

151. Bei jemand auf dem Kerbholz stehen. *To be indebted to somebody.*

152. Das Kind beim rechten Namen nennen. *To talk plainly. To call a spade a spade.*

153. Etwas aufs Korn nehmen. *To call attention to something,* or *to have one's eye on something.*

154. Frisch von der Leber sprechen. *To speak frankly.*

155. Lehrgeld geben. *To pay dearly for experience.*

156. Über einen Leisten schlagen. *To do everything in the same manner.*

157. Schuster bleib' bei deinem Leisten! *Cobbler stick to your last. Stick to your trade.*

158. Zu guter letzt. *Finally.*

159. Auf dem letzten Loche pfeifen. *To be breathing one's last.*

160. Einen Narren an jemand gefressen haben. *To be foolishly captivated by a person.*

161. Die Nase rümpfen. *To stick up one's nose.*

162. Er is naseweis. *He is inquisitive.*

163. Es hinter den Ohren haben. *To be shrewd, cunning.*

164. Aus dem Regen in die Traufe. *From the frying pan into the fire.*

165. In Saus und Braus leben. *To live high.*

166. Etwas im Schilde führen. *To plan something secretly.*

167. Er schlägt seiner Mutter nach. *He resembles his mother.*

168. Reden, wie einem der Schnabel gewachsen ist. *To speak one's mind freely.*

169. Zeter und Mord schreien. *To raise an outcry.*

170. Er hat sein Schäfchen ins Trockene gebracht. *He has had good luck.*

171. Er weiss wo Barthold den Most holt. *He knows the ropes.*

172. Gegen jemand in die Schranken treten. *To take a stand openly against a person.*

173. Eine Scharte auswetzen. *To wipe out an old score.*

174. In Bausch und Bogen. *In a lump.*

175. Jemandem etwas einbrocken. *To serve a person an ill turn.*

176. Bei dem ist eine Schraube los. *He is beside himself. There is a screw loose.*

177. Gesichter schneiden. *To make faces.*

178. Er ist von altem Schrot und Korn. *He is of genuine German stock.*

179. Einem ins Gehege kommen. *To put a spoke in one's wheel.*

180. Die Schule schwänzen. *To run away from school. To cut classes.*

181. Das ändert an der Sache gar nichts. *That makes no difference.*

182. Auf Schusters Rappen gehen. *To go on foot.*

183. Seine sieben Sachen packen. *To pack up and leave with a few belongings.*

184. Er hat einen Sparren zu viel. *He is not mentally well balanced.*

185. Er ist in voller Wichse. *He is all togged out.*

186. Über jemand den Stab brechen. *To condemn a person.*

187. Einem den Stuhl vor die Tür setzen. *To throw a person out of the house.*

188. Er giebt sich damit zufrieden. *He is satisfied.*

189. Warten, dass einem die gebratenen Tauben in den Mund fliegen. *Waiting to take life easy, to obtain something without effort.*

190. Die Grillen vertreiben. *To drive away the blues.*

191. Sich mit Grillen plagen. *To brood over one's troubles.*

192. Er hat den Ton angegeben. *He sets the pace.*

193. Mäkele nicht zu viel. *Do not find too much fault.*

194. Umstände machen. *To make much ado about nothing.*

195. Den Wald vor lauter Bäume nicht sehen. *Not to see the woods for the trees.*

196. Jemand beim Fittich erwischen. *To collar or buttonhole a person.*

197. Jemandem standhalten. *To hold out against a person.*

198. Einem nicht das Wasser reichen. *He can not hold a candle to him.*

199. Die Gelegenheit beim Schopfe fassen. *To improve the opportunity.*

200. Er stellte sie zur Rede. *He called them to account.*

201. Sich ein X für ein U machen lassen. *To be bamboozled.*

202. Er machte einen Fleischergang. *He went on a fool's errand.*

203. Er wittert Unrat. *He smells a rat.*

204. Etwas in Abrede stellen, ziehen. *To deny.*

205. In die Richte gehen. *To take the shortest cut.*

206. Der fährt hoch her. *He comes in great style.*

207. Eine Bewegung fasst Fuss. *A movement is on foot.*

208. Er kennt die Schliche. *He knows the tricks of the trade.*

209. Da sitzt der Knoten. *Here lies the trouble.*

210. Die Kosten überschlagen. *To count the cost.*

211. Das Hasenpanier ergreifen. *To take to one's heels.*

212. Viel auf Anstand halten. *To have a great regard for propriety.*

213. Es beliebt mir. *I choose, it pleases me.*

214. Im Rufe stehn. *To have the reputation.*

215. Jemandem das Gleichgewicht halten. *To hold one's own with some one.*

216. Um so besser. *So much the better.*

217. Ich bin Ihnen sehr verbunden. *I am very much obliged to you.*

218. Ein Backfisch. *A girl in her teens.*

219. Einer (eine) aus der siebenten Bitte. *An obnoxious person.*

220. Einen blauen Dunst vor die Augen machen. *To pull the wool over one's eyes.*

221. Sich nach der Decke strecken. *To cut one's coat according to one's cloth.*

222. Die Flinte ins Korn werfen. *To lose courage.*

223. Fünf gerade sein lassen. *Not too particular.*

224. Einem den roten Hahn aufs Dach setzen. *To set one's house on fire.*

225. An dem ist Hopfen und Malz verloren. *He is a hopeless case.*

ABBREVIATIONS

a. a. O.—am angeführten Orte.

A. G.—Aktien Gesellschaft.

ahd.—althochdeutsch.

allg.—allgemein.

A. T.—Altes Testament.

betr.—betreffend.

bspw.—beispielsweise.

bzw.—beziehungsweise.

dergl. (dgl.)—dergleichen.

d. h.—das heisst.

d. i.—das ist.

d. J.—dieses Jahres.

e. g.—zum Beispiel.

eig.—eigentlich.

etw.—etwas.

Ew.—Euer or Eure.

f. (ff.)—folgende.

fg.—folgendes.

geb.—geboren.

gest.—gestorben.

gew.—gewöhnlich.

hd.—hochdeutsch.

Hoh.—Hoheit

Hr.—Herr.

i. allg.—im allgemeinen.

i. J.—im Jahr.

Jh.—Jahrhundert.

M.—Mark.

mhd.—mittelhochdeutsch.

n. Chr.—nach Christo.

nhd.—neuhochdeutsch.

N. N.—(Mr.) So and So.

N. T.—Neues Testament.

O.—Ort.

o. (od.)—oder.

Pf.—Pfennige.

S.—Seite.

s.—siehe.

S. M.—Seine Majestät.

sog.—sogenannt.

Thlr.—Thaler.

u.—und.

u. a.—unter anderem.

u. a. m.—und andere mehr.

U. A. w. g.—Um Antwort wird gebeten.

u. dergl.—und dergleichen.

u. s. f.—und so fort.

u. s. w.—und so weiter.

v.—von.

v. Chr.—vor Christo.

vergl. (vgl.)—vergleiche.

v. J.—vorigen Jahres.

z. B.—zum Beispiel.

Money, Weights, and Measures

A comparison of money in Germany, France, England, and the United States.

One Dollar = 4.1979 Marks = 5.1826 Francs = .20 Pound.
One Mark = 100 Pfennig = 1.24 Francs = 11¾ Pence = $0.24.
Krone = 10 Marks (gold coin).   Thaler = 3 Marks.

Approximate Metric Equivalents.

1 decimeter . 4 inches	1 liter (liquid) . . . . 1.06 qt.
1 meter . . 1.1 yard	" (dry) . . . . . .9 qt.
1 kilometer . ⅝ mile	1 kilogram . . . . 2 1-5 lbs.

The Metric System is used all over Germany.
Other useful weights and measures.

Morgen . . . 180 sq. rods   Schock . . . . 60 pieces
Mandel . . . 15 pieces   Stiege . . . . 20 pieces
Pfund (no longer official) . . . . 500 Grams.

INDEX

239

MAP OF
THE GERMAN EMPIRE
AND ADJACENT COUNTRIES
TO ILLUSTRATE
Holzwarth's Students' Manual
SCALE OF MILES
0   25   50   75   100

REFERENCE
S.C.G. = Saxe-Coburg-Gotha,
S.W. = Saxe-Weimar.
S.A. = Saxe-Altenburg.
S.M. = Saxe-Meiningen.
S.S. = Schwarzburg-Sondershausen.
S.R. = Schwarzburg-Rudolstadt.
R.G. = Reuss-Greiz.
R.G. = Reuss-Gera
S.L. = Schaumburg-Lippe.

GERMAN TEXTS

INTERMEDIATE

AMERICAN BOOK COMPANY

(S. 224)

GERMAN TEXTS

ELEMENTARY

AMERICAN BOOK COMPANY

TWO GERMAN READERS

By MENCO STERN

Geschichten vom Rhein $0.85
Geschichten von Deutschen Städten.   In two Parts.
    Each 70

THESE two collections of stories are designed to arouse and stimulate the pupil's interest, not only while he is struggling with the difficulties of German grammar, but even after he has successfully completed the study.   They make him acquainted with the German people, and describe faithfully the various sections of the German Empire.

¶ The books furnish interesting reading matter, and include, besides, valuable suggestive material for exercises in conversation and composition.   While each chapter is complete in itself, yet, taken together, they form a complete whole, and afford a good general acquaintance with the scenes in which they are laid.   In Geschichten von Deutschen Städten, the stories commence with the cities on the coast of the North Sea, and progress through the leading towns of the German Empire.   In Geschichten vom Rhein, the reader starts from the source of the Rhine, and follows it throughout its course.   These sketches all portray the romance of Germany — its scenery, cities, castles, and homes, interweaving with the descriptions the legends and folklore of the people.   They do not, however, consist of fiction only, but furnish also many facts of historical, geographical, and literary importance.   The carefully compiled vocabularies furnish ample aid.   The maps help show the significance of the tales.

AMERICAN   BOOK   COMPANY

(S. 225)

GERMAN PROSE COMPOSITION

By CARL W. J. OSTHAUS, Professor of German, Indiana
University; and ERNEST H. BIERMANN, Instructor
in German, Indiana University. Price, 65 cents.

THE work in this book is based on consecutive prose,
and is intended to develop rapidly the student's sense
of independence. The selections are really new and
fresh, and offer a wide range of material, being anecdotal
and historical, taken from Germanic folklore, literature,
and real life.

¶ A portion of the elementary exercises is made up of three
parts: a German selection, a set of questions in German,
and an English paraphrase of the preceding German selection for translation into German. The German selection
forms the basis of the work which follows, and should be
studied thoroughly before the translation is worked out by
the class. In the elementary part most of the selections
are preceded by a statement of the grammatical principles
involved, thus making it easy for the instructor to assign
certain portions of grammar for review.

¶ The questions in German, which are intended to be
answered in German, afford excellent practice work in the
transposition of tenses or persons, and the changing from
direct to indirect discourse, etc. As the selections increase
in length the questions are omitted. Copious footnotes
throughout the book provide the needful suggestions and
refer the student to sections of the digest of syntax which
follows the text. This digest, which is intended chiefly for
the guidance of the inexperienced, is to be supplemented
by the grammar with which the student is familiar. There
are full German-English and English-German vocabularies
at the end of the book.

AMERICAN BOOK COMPANY

(S.227)

FOUNDATIONS OF GERMAN

By C. F. KAYSER, Ph. D., Professor of German, Normal
College of the City of New York ; and F. MONTESER,
Ph. D., Head of German Department, De Witt Clinton
High School, New York.   Price, 80 cents.

THIS course reduces to a minimum all preparatory
work, and introduces the learner at the earliest possible moment to the literature of the language.
Among its distinctive features are :

I. It includes only topics absolutely essential for any
progress whatever, and it presents them as briefly as is
consistent with perfect clearness.

II. It makes large use of " the living grammar." In
this way it enlivens instruction in grammar, stimulates
self-activity, and develops the feeling for correctness,
which is the chief thing to be looked for in all language
study.

III. It lends itself excellently to conversational practice.
The vocabulary has been selected very carefully from everyday language, and the German exercises are all of a colloquial and strictly idiomatic character, so that they may
be turned into impromptu conversation.   This is still more
true of the connected readings, which are very simple.

IV. It offers a firm foundation on which a solid super-
structure can be erected.   The lessons are steadily progres-
sive; no attempt is made to minimize difficulties at the
beginning.   The English exercises give the pupil a chance
to test his knowledge and power, while the exercises in
word formation stimulate his interest in the building up of
his vocabulary, which will be of great service in future
sight reading.

AMERICAN   BOOK   COMPANY
(S.229)

FRANÇOIS' ESSENTIALS
OF FRENCH

By VICTOR E. FRANÇOIS, Ph.D., Associate Professor of French, College of the City of New York

90 cents

A COURSE for beginners, whose acquirement of a foreign language is often hampered by an incomplete mastery of English grammar. The development here proceeds from the known English form to the unknown French form, with constant comparison and contrast.

¶ The models precede the rules, the salient features being made prominent by heavy type. The rules cover the necessary facts of the language as simply and completely as possible, but the student is not confused by masses of exceptions, peculiarities, and idioms rarely seen and still more rarely used. The vocabulary, of moderate extent, is composed of ordinary words likely to be used in everyday conversation, and is increased slowly, care being taken to repeat the words again and again in succeeding exercises.

¶ The first lessons have been made short and simple, in order to allow for the initial difficulties. The exercises are composed of sentences connected in sense so far as this is possible without detriment to the application of the principles and repetition of words. Each lesson includes generally four exercises: a review, a portion of French text, a set of questions based on the text and usually followed by a grammar drill, and an English exercise based on the text and on the rules developed in the lesson.

AMERICAN BOOK COMPANY
(S. 220)

FRENCH TEXTS

THESE French texts are, in the main, those which are read most by classes following the recommendations of the Modern Language Association, the College Entrance Examination Board, and the New York State Education Department. In addition a few others are included which are no less suitable.

ELEMENTARY

AMERICAN BOOK COMPANY
(S. 216)

FRENCH TEXTS

THESE French texts are, in the main, those which are read most by classes following the recommendations of the Modern Language Association.

INTERMEDIATE

ADVANCED

AMERICAN BOOK COMPANY

(S. 217)

FRENCH COMPOSITIONS

By H. A. GUERBER

EASY FRENCH PROSE COMPOSITION
$0.25

THIS prose composition is based on Guerber's Contes et Légendes, Part I, which it is planned to accompany. The exercises consist of English parallel versions of each of the twenty-five selections, with the necessary indications of the correct renderings. Suggestions are afforded regarding words to be omitted and others which will aid in the translation. No vocabulary is included, since the pupil will find in the original text all the data necessary. The principle of constant repetition found in the stories is applied throughout the exercises.

JOAN OF ARC—FRENCH COMPOSITION
$0.30

THE composition work in this book is based on the principle that the best results can be obtained through the use of material which is both interesting and consecutive. The life and exploits of Joan of Arc are presented in the form of a continuous narrative, which is written in an agreeable style, and adapted especially to the purpose in view. Copious foot-notes, indicating by rearrangement of the English words the equivalent French construction, and a full vocabulary are included.

AMERICAN BOOK COMPANY
(S.219)

ESSENTIALS OF SPANISH GRAM-
MAR $1.00

By SAMUEL GARNER, Ph. D., formerly Professor of Modern Languages, U. S. Naval Academy.

IN this work only such features of the grammatical mechanism are treated as are essential for the reading of ordinary Spanish. Besides the clear exposition of grammar and syntax, the book includes exercises combining drill upon grammatical points with practice in translation and pronunciation, and at the same time provides ample work in memorizing. All the exercises are new, and are incorporated in the text. Special vocabularies accompany the first ten lessons.

SPANISH PROSE COMPOSITION, $0.75

By G. W. UMPHREY, Ph.D., Assistant Professor of Romance Languages, University of Cincinnati.

THIS book offers interesting material systematically arranged for translation, composition, and conversation in Spanish. The lessons are so arranged that besides offering material for conversation and exercises in translation, they afford an opportunity for systematic review of all the essentials of Spanish grammar. The exercises are varied in character and lead up to independent translation from English into Spanish and to original composition in Spanish.

AMERICAN BOOK COMPANY

(S 232)

SPANISH TEXTS

E ACH volume of these Spanish texts contains notes and a vocabulary.

WORMAN'S SPANISH BOOKS — REVISED

| First Spanish Book. $0.40 | Second Spanish Book . $0.40 |

I N their new form these books offer a satisfactory course in spoken Spanish. The FIRST BOOK teaches directly by illustration, contrast, association, and natural inference. The exercises grow out of pictured objects and actions, and the words are kept so constantly in mind that no translation or use of English is required to fix their meaning. In the SECOND BOOK the accentuation agrees with the latest rules of the language.

AMERICAN BOOK COMPANY
(S. 233)

DESCRIPTIVE CATALOGUE OF HIGH SCHOOL AND COLLEGE TEXTBOOKS

Published Complete and in Sections

WE issue a Catalogue of High School and College Textbooks, which we have tried to make as valuable and as useful to teachers as possible. In this catalogue are set forth briefly and clearly the scope and leading characteristics of each of our best textbooks. In most cases there are also given testimonials from well-known teachers, which have been selected quite as much for their descriptive qualities as for their value as commendations.

¶ For the convenience of teachers this Catalogue is also published in separate sections treating of the various branches of study. These pamphlets are entitled: English, Mathematics, History and Political Science, Science, Modern Foreign Languages, Ancient Languages, Commercial Subjects and Philosophy and Education. A separate pamphlet is devoted to the Newest Books in all subjects.

¶ Teachers seeking the newest and best books for their classes are invited to send for any of these.

¶ Copies of our price lists, or of special circulars, in which these books are described at greater length than the space limitations of the catalogue permit, will be mailed to any address on request. Address all correspondence to the nearest office of the company.

AMERICAN BOOK COMPANY
(S.312)